KNOW
&
GROW

KNOW
&
GROW

Volume 2

by
Cheryl Fawcett

REGULAR BAPTIST PRESS
1300 North Meacham Road
Post Office Box 95500
Schaumburg, Illinois 60195

To my mother, Lydia, whose "heart the Lord opened" and
who first opened my heart to the Lord Jesus.

Library of Congress Cataloging in Publication Data

Fawcett, Cheryl, 1953–
  Know and grow.

  1. Sunday-schools—Exercises, recitations, etc.
I. Title.
BV1570.F38   1982   268'.4   82-21567
ISBN 0-87227-086-6 (v. 1)
ISBN 0-87227-090-4 (v. 2)

© 1983
Regular Baptist Press
Schaumburg, Illinois
Printed in U.S.A.

CONTENTS

WHO IS JESUS CHRIST?

PREFACE

This book contains over 30 devotionals for children from basic Bible texts. It is written for the teacher of children and includes specific instructions on visual aids and applications to the life of the learner. Each lesson has aims directed toward the learner that are specific, measurable and attainable.

The intent of the book is to help children study the Bible themselves, with the teacher as a guide. Too many children have been given second-hand spiritual food. They can learn Bible doctrine and truths directly from Bible texts with the careful help of a prepared teacher.

It is my desire not only to provide teaching material for teachers of grade school children, but also to help them develop a personal involvement in Bible research for themselves and their pupils.

— *Cheryl Fawcett*

I Have More Questions

WHO IS CHRIST?

Scripture Text: *"And Simon Peter answered and said, Thou art the Christ, the Son of the living God" (Matt. 16:16).*

Lesson Aim: The student will be able to give Peter's response to the lesson's question. The student will be given opportunity to answer the question for himself.

Are You Ready?

Have you ever played "Who Am I?" An individual takes on the identity of someone else. He describes the character and actions of this special someone, and others try to guess who is being described. It is a fun game, challenging listeners to think, evaluate and finally propose a name or two. The harder it is to guess, the more the enjoyment. The identity of the secret person is important to all who play.

You and I have a need to know who people are. If we walk into a room and see a stranger, we would most likely ask, "Who is that?" If we are new, we like to be introduced so we know who we are with. A person's name and title often give us valuable information for our conversation and relationship.

Our lesson today centers around the question, "Who am I?"

See for Yourself

Open your Bible to the Gospel of Matthew. It is the first book of the New Testament. Matthew wrote this account of the birth, life, death and resurrection of Jesus. We will study chapter 16, beginning at verse 13. Read with me verses 13 through 16. Notice where Jesus was and who was with Him.

Verse 13 tells us that Jesus had gone where? Yes, He was in the district of Caesarea Philippi. It is north of the Sea of Galilee near the foot of Mount Hermon. Who was with Jesus on this journey? His twelve close followers, the disciples. Of all the people who had seen or been with Jesus, these men knew Him best. They had traveled together for several years. Jesus had talked plainly and openly to them about Himself.

Now Jesus asks an important question. It is written down in verse 13. Read the question out loud to all of us, please. "Whom do men say that I the Son of man am?" It is a "Who Am I?" question. He is not asking, at this point, the disciples' perception. Rather He asks, "Whom do *men* say that I am?" The disciples would know this since the people talked openly with them about this man they followed.

They give four answers. What are they? Verse 14 lists John the Baptist, Elias, Jeremiah, one of the prophets. Who was John the Baptist? (*Allow time for students to respond, filling in if they omit important details.*) John the Baptist was Jesus' cousin. He was a forerunner or announcer to point men to Jesus. He sounded much like Jesus because he proclaimed the same message. Some folks must have confused Jesus with John. Elias or Elijah was a man of miracles who was reported to come to life again. Jesus did miracles, the people were thinking, so maybe He was Elijah back from the dead. Jeremiah was one of the well-known prophets of Israel. He had many messages for the people from God, so some thought Jesus to be Jeremiah. Others weren't so specific. He is a prophet, they said, but they were not sure which one. The ideas of the crowd were varied. They really weren't certain who Jesus was.

Jesus' next question is more specific. What is the question and why is it more pointed? Verse 15 will help you. It says, "Who do you [my twelve disciples] say that I am?" This question is more personal. It requires an individual answer.

Peter spoke up and responded to Jesus' inquiry. Peter was the spokesman for the group—their unofficial leader. His answer revealed his own personal belief as well as that of his friends. Notice that his answer is singular. When the disciples answered for the crowd they gave four answers; now there was room for only one.

Give the two parts of Peter's title for Jesus. First, He is *the* Christ. Second, He is the Son of the living God. "Christ" means the anointed One—He was the One promised by God to be King. He didn't act like other kings they knew, but Peter titled Him King! The second statement ties Jesus to God as His Son. There were many false gods and idols in that day. Peter identified Christ as the *living* Son of God. Other gods were powerless to help or intervene in their worshipers' lives. Not this God—He is living!

Live It

The question is: Who do others say Jesus is? The answers in Bible times and in our day are many and varied. Many misunderstand, confuse and distort His identity.

The second question is for you as well as for the Twelve. Who do you say this Jesus is? Are you confused? Disappointed? Do you personally believe what you know to be true? Is He your Christ?

Have you allowed Him to be the monarch, the ruling power in your life? Do you know Him as the Son of the living and powerful God? If not, you may do so today. He wants to be *your* Christ and your link to the living God of Heaven.

If He is yours, have you openly told others? Peter was willing to speak up, not only for himself but for others. You may need to begin in a circumstance where you are with others who claim Him as Lord. That's not wrong—but do tell others who may not know Him Who you believe Jesus to be.

To the Instructor: Make It Visual

For the opening session you may wish to play a round or two of "Who Am I?" This will give students the seed thought of today's lesson.

A series of flashcards can be easily made from poster board or heavy construction paper to illustrate the basic points of the lesson. See diagram below for help.

Q	WHO IS CHRIST?	A	JOHN THE BAPTIST	ELIJAH
JEREMIAH	PROPHETS	YOU	YOU	

WHAT IS GOD'S GIFT?

Scripture Text: *"For the wages of sin is death; but the gift of God is eternal life through Jesus Christ our Lord" (Rom. 6:23).*

Lesson Aim: The student will be able to tell that God's gift is life that never ends. The student will be able to explain that eternal life is a gift: it is not earned, it must be received.

Are You Ready?

Think of a gift that you have received that meant a lot to you. Tell us what it was and why you choose that gift to talk about now. Would you prefer receiving gifts that you really need or gifts that you have no use for? Does it make any difference who gives the gift? If someone you think a lot of gives you a gift, it adds value to the gift. The cost of a gift is important, too. What the giver has and what he is willing to share is part of the value of the gift.

Each of us likes to receive a gift. Today we are seeking to answer the question, "What is God's gift?" We will study two verses that describe the gift. This gift is for YOU! It is something you really need. It is from God Himself and was very costly.

See for Yourself

Open your Bible to Romans 6:23 and fill in the missing

words from this verse. "For the _____ of sin is _____ but the _____ ____ _____ is _____ _____ through Jesus Christ our Lord." (*Allow enough time for all to complete the verse.*) The missing words are, in order: wages, death, gift of God, eternal life. Not only are those the missing words, but they are key words in the verse. Let's talk about each one briefly.

What is a wage? A wage is pay for work done. You earn it. If your dad works so many hours doing a task assigned by his job in an acceptable manner, he earns a wage. It belongs to him. It must be paid to him.

What is the wage this verse describes? This is a difficult question, so take time to read the verse again. Death is the wage. We all know what death is. The word here is very strong—it means to cut off. It is sudden and final. Once this wage is paid there is no giving it back or changing your mind.

What must we do to earn this wage? The verse says that if we *sin,* we will receive the wage of death. Sin is any thought, word or deed contrary to God's will. I've sinned many times; so have you. Do you want your wage? I don't! And neither do you if you are wise and serious about it.

The gift of God comes next in this verse. Aren't you glad? You and I really need God's gift. It will deliver us from danger. It is free! You haven't received a genuine gift if you pay something for it. We are in danger of death, but God's gift will deliver us from death. What a gift!

Now, to the question we need to answer today. What is God's gift? It is eternal life. Eternal life is perpetual, or life that goes on and on and on. It isn't cut off—that would be death. This is life and it is forever. What a gift! It is free to you, though it was very costly to God.

Ephesians 2:8 tells us that by grace we are saved. It is not of ourselves but it is the gift of God. It is God's gift to us.

Live It

The post office has a dead letter department. It consists of all the letters that were written but for a variety of reasons weren't delivered. The postal service also has freight offices for undeliverable materials. Someone paid for the goods. They were to be delivered but they never got to their owners. They are gifts given but not received.

God's gift is paid for. Your eternal life was paid for in full when Jesus died on the cross, was buried and came to life again. You don't have to receive your wage of death. God's gift of life that never ends is yours if you will receive it as a gift. Don't try to earn it or try to pay God back. It is a gift, a gift you really need. Receive it today. Tell the Lord you are thankful.

To the Instructor: Make It Visual

Write the text for today, with the appropriate words omitted, on either the chalkboard, an overhead, a poster board or on individual sheets for each student.

Bring an attractively wrapped gift to class. It will be useful for gaining attention in the opening moments. Everyone has enough curiosity to want to know what is inside. You should be able to obtain a poster with the minimum wage listed from an employer or government agency. Post this in a conspicuous place for all to see. Contrast a gift and the wage.

WHY DO I SIN?

Scripture Text: *"The heart is deceitful above all things, and desperately wicked: who can know it?" (Jer. 17:9).*

Lesson Aim: The student will be able to tell that he sins because of a crooked heart. The student will select from this list the origin of wrong (italicized responses are correct answers): drugs, movies, books, TV, friends, *inside not outside,* radio, bad neighbors, *heart, wicked thoughts.*

Are You Ready?

Please meet Sally Ordinary. She is continually in trouble at home and at school and she doesn't go to church anymore. When she did go she made trouble there, too. When asked why she sins, Sally has many reasons. You see, she watches some really bad TV shows. Her choice of music isn't the best—in fact, her mother won't allow it in the house. If things weren't bad enough, last summer Sally made friends with some kids who were on drugs. Eventually Sally was experimenting with drugs herself.

If we could take away all of these bad influences from Sally, would she sin? What do you think and, more importantly, why do you think that? (*This discussion is vital to the lesson to let the teacher know what the student believes to be the origin of sin. Guide the discussion; don't stifle it.*)

Now how about you? What makes you sin? Is it the bad influences around you? The bad people and questionable activities that make you do wrong? Why do you and I sin?

See for Yourself

Fill in these blanks, using your Bible. Jeremiah 17:9: "The _____ is _____ above all things and _____ _____: who can know it?" Isaiah 64:6: "But we are all as an _____ _____, and all our _____ are as _____ _____; and we all do fade as a leaf; and our _____ like the wind, have taken us away." (*For the sake of time you may assign separate groups to complete each verse. Then as they exchange answers, they benefit from each other's work.*) You should have these words: heart, deceitful, desperately, wicked; unclean, thing, righteousnesses, filthy, rags, iniquities.

Each of the words in the answer is a key to understanding these verses and the question we are attempting to answer. You can probably guess pretty closely what most of them mean. After you do your best, I will give you any assistance needed. Ready?

What is your heart? Not the organ that pumps your blood but the center of you—your inside decision-maker. Now, how is this decision-maker described? Yes, it is deceitful. "Deceitful" means crooked or polluted. A crooked stick can't be made straight without breaking it, nor a polluted river made pure without extensive cleaning. What other two words describe your heart? If you said "desperately wicked" you are absolutely correct! What is another way to say that? Continually wrong, constantly rotten; or, literally, it means incurably evil.

With that sort of a heart, what kinds of choices will you and I make nearly all the time? Why? We will make wrong, evil, sinful decisions. What else could we possibly do?

Before we move to our Isaiah verse, one more comment. The verse implies that our heart is so crooked that at times even we don't know what it's up to. How can you control a heart like that? You can't. And just add those bad outside influences, and your heart will pick only sinful options.

Now, to Isaiah 64:6. How are we described here? It says we are, all of us included here, as an unclean thing. We are foul, polluted. Not the kind of person you would want to be around. How about our best efforts? When we really shine and do our nicest niceties, how do we measure up with God? We look like a heap of soiled rags. Our best is only rags with God.

The word "iniquities" means evil or sins. It could read this way: Our sins take us away from God just like a wind blows away crumpled leaves in the fall. That's not a very good picture. It is a truthful one, though, and we need to know the truth.

Finally, read with me through both verses again (Jer. 17:9 and Isa. 64:6). As we do, consider our question for today: "Why do I sin?"

Live It

Can you answer the question now? You and I sin continually because we have heart trouble. Our heart is crooked, polluted, rotten. This kind of a heart is incapable of making sound, pure, straight decisions and actions. Our problem is not the friends around us, the TV, the radio, or the temptation to use drugs. Those things don't help us, but we choose to do wrong because of our evil heart. Jesus said it so clearly to the Scribes and Pharisees. They were really upset with Jesus' disciples because the disciples had forgotten to wash their hands before eating. In Matthew 15:18-20 He concludes that dirty hands don't make a person sinful.

Sin is a matter of the heart. "But those things which proceed out of the mouth come forth from the heart; and they defile [make him dirty] the man."

Why do you sin? Don't blame your friends, environment or parents. Jeremiah 17:9 says you and your heart are responsible. Admit your sinfulness to God today and ask for forgiveness.

To the Instructor: Make It Visual

Be sure to have extra Bibles available for students who don't have one. It is of much more value for them to see the answers than for you to tell them. They will remember what they find much better and *much* longer.

You will have to have written out on the chalkboard, bulletin board, overhead or poster board the two verses that serve as the key here (Jeremiah 17:9 and Isaiah 64:6). If you don't like lettering, the stationery store has stencils available. Your library may also have patterns for letters. You are without excuse if you teach without visual reinforcement.

A magazine picture will work nicely to introduce Sally. Mount the picture on construction paper with Elmer's glue or rubber cement.

If you have use of an overhead projector, a series of transparency visuals is given below.

HOW CAN I PLEASE GOD?

Scripture Text: *"Not by works of righteousness which we have done . . ." (Titus 3:5).*
"But to him that . . . believeth on him that justifieth the ungodly, his faith is counted for righteousness" (Rom. 4:5).

Lesson Aim: The student will be able to tell what God's standard is (a holy life) and what man is (sinful, crooked, polluted). The student will be able to answer that faith pleases God, *not* works or self-effort.

Are You Ready?

Please watch closely the following situations that show young people making efforts to please someone. Who are they trying to please and will they succeed? *(Arrange for help to act these out prior to class time.)*

Situation 1: Sally and Janice are getting ready for their class party. Sally: How does my new hairstyle look? Janice: Oh, Sally, it's really beautiful. I think Mark will really like it. Here, let me just touch up this curl over here. There . . . oh, it is nice. Sally: Do you think he will notice?

Situation 2: Greg and Brad are in the locker room near their high school swimming pool. Greg: I've got to take two seconds off my time by Friday! Brad: Why the big push, Greg? Greg: Oh, Coach Fisher says I can't go to the meet in Upsdale unless I can swim the fifty meters faster. I really want to be in that meet. What can I do? Brad: Why don't you do extra laps after practice. That may ease Coach's mind and it could help strengthen your stroke and cut your time. Greg: It's worth a try, I guess. Sure do hope I make it.

See for Yourself

The girls were trying to please a particular fellow. It is hard to know if they will please him or not. The standard is arbitrary. Greg wants to please his coach. He knows exactly what he must do to accomplish that. Whether he pleases the coach or not depends on whether he reaches the time goal.

God wants something from you and me. His standard is very clearly given in the Bible. You may read it in Leviticus 11:44: ". . . Ye shall be holy; for I am holy." The standard is easy to read; difficult, seemingly impossible to live. "Holy" means to be separated from *all* that is sinful or impure; to be perfect. Our world and our lives are polluted with sin, with impure thoughts, impure deeds and less than perfect actions. We are people given to selfishness, envy, pride, greed, anger, and on and on we could go.

What does God want from us? He wants us to be holy. Can you recall from our last lesson on Jeremiah 17:9, "The heart is deceitful above all things . . . ," and Isaiah 64:6, "We are all as an unclean thing . . ."? What did we learn about the condition of man? We are sinful, crooked, polluted. There is nothing in us or that comes out of us that comes anywhere near to God's call to be holy.

What was our question today? How can I please God? Once you know what it takes to be holy, you instantly know that there's nothing you can do to measure up to a standard like that.

Listen carefully to the first part of Titus 3:5. It tells how we *can't* please God. What way will not work? "Not by works of righteousness which we have done. . . ." Our work, deeds, toil, labors count for nothing. Sounds like the only thing to do

25

is to throw our hands up in defeat and live any way we want to; we can't please God anyway. But wait! That's not right.

Open your Bible to Titus 3:5 and Romans 4:5.

The word "but" jumps out in contrast. Our works don't count, but God's mercy does. Mercy means compassion. By His compassion, His undeserved kindness, we are saved.

Fill in these blanks: "But to him that _____ not, but _____ on him that _____ the ungodly, his _____ is counted for _____ ." Your answers should be worketh, believeth, justifieth, faith, righteousness. Again the contrast is presented. Can you see it? Point it out. No to works, yes to faith. Works don't do you any good in earning favor with God. By placing trust in Jesus and His mercy toward you, you can have His holy record for your own. God specializes in making unholy men holy. Working won't get you anywhere. Placing your faith in the Lord Jesus will.

Live It

What is God's standard? A holy life. What is man's record? Sinful, polluted, crooked, trying to work to please God. What does please God according to Romans 4:5? Think carefully. You may have been taught differently. Make sure your answer comes straight from the Bible—that's God's Word and is always accurate. Faith counts for righteousness or a holy life. You will have to exchange your life for God's holy life if you are ever to please Him.

Have you accepted Jesus' death and resurrection for your own life? Does His mercy count for you? Today is the day to please God!

To the Instructor: Make It Visual

Prepare three posters with the key questions of the lesson. Also prepare Scriptural references with the appropriate responses. Prepare a poster board or chalkboard with Romans 4:5 and the appropriate words and blanks. This lesson is vital for students to see for themselves. Many have been taught that they *can* please God by working, through self-effort. It will take repeated instruction and careful explanation for them to realize the distinction you are teaching. Be patient and careful and don't give up until they get it!

GOD WANTS	LEV. 11:44
MAN IS	JER. 17:9 IS. 64:6
PLEASE GOD	TITUS 3:5 ROM. 4:5

WHY MEMORIZE THE BIBLE?

Scripture Text: *"Thy word have I hid in mine heart, that I might not sin against thee" (Ps. 119:11).*

Lesson Aim: The student will be able to name three of the five reasons why memory work is important. The student will choose to memorize or not to memorize a verse this week.

Are You Ready?

Who can tell me what three times three equals? Yes, nine. How about two plus two? It equals four, of course. What is the capital of our state? What is the nation's capital?

Did you have to look at a times table to know the answer to three times three? Why? You memorized that in grade school. How many used their fingers to add two and two? No one, because you had done it so many times that you remembered without a lot of thinking. It sort of "jumped" into your mind when I asked the question.

There are many things that we memorize either purposely or just by continual use. These are the items of information that are necessary for the tasks we do every day. All of us can memorize. Some things are easier to remember than others. The twelve times tables are not as easy to remember as your favorite piano piece or favorite baseball players' statistics. It is true that we do remember easier, longer and better what we *want* to remember.

Today we will talk about *why* we work to memorize the Bible. If you understand the "why," the "how-to" will be easier. Are you ready?

See for Yourself

Today we will explore five reasons for Bible memorization. They are all found in the same Bible book, Psalms. They all appear in the 119th chapter. Open your Bible to Psalm 119. We will begin at verse 9.

Read the verse out loud with me. It is written in a question and answer format. The question tells us a reason *why* we should be memorizing the Bible. What is it? It helps to cleanse a young man's way. We might ask, "How can a young man keep his life pure?" You fall into the category of "young man" in this verse. It means one from infancy through teen years. You are young. You can keep your way or life pure and clean by paying attention to the Word of God. The best way to pay attention to something is to know it so well that you have instant recall. In other words, the first reason for memorizing God's Word is *so your life will be clean.*

The first reason is a positive reason. It is directed to help you keep your life going on the right track. The second reason is similar but stated in a reversed manner. Look for it in 119:11. What is it? *Memorize so that you will not sin.* The word "hid" means to hoard, to reserve in a safe place. You have heard stories about misers who hoard money. Scrooge was a man like that. He kept every gold coin he could get his hands on. A miser guards what he has as though there will never be any more. He isn't going to allow even one coin to slip through his hands. You and I need to be the same way with God's Word. We need to hoard it away to the safe places of our memory. The Bible can be taken from your hands, but no one has direct access to your mind. Hide God's Word there for it will be safe and will keep you from sin.

Reason three is in verse 98 of the same chapter. Read it aloud. If you memorize Scripture, *you will be wiser than your enemies!* That's as good as a victory!

We won't be able to get rid of enemies in life (see that in the second half of the verse). But we can outsmart them. What makes us wiser than our enemies? The psalm writer, David, says that through the commandments of God we are wise. When we memorize the commands of God, we become wise in thought as they invade our thinking, our words and our actions. Do you want to be wise? Then memorize Scripture and you will be *wiser than your enemies.*

Verse 99 follows right along. It is a personal testimony, true of David's life. It can be true of yours, too, if you'll do what he did. How do you know from this verse that he memorized? It says, "thy testimonies are my meditation." The word "meditation" means to reflect, think back over, to ponder, to talk with yourself aloud, to babble. That's a humorous definition. It sounds a lot like a memorizing session, doesn't it? Talking out loud, babbling, saying a verse over and over until you have it and then over and over until it has you. What did all of that do for David? It caused him to have more understanding than his teachers. He had better insight to see things as they really were because of his memory work. Ah, you say, I'd love to be smarter than my schoolteacher! That's not what David is saying. Remember, teachers are smart because they, too, took time to learn what you are now learning. But if you will spend time memorizing the Bible, you can *have more insight than your teachers.* It's a challenge. How about it?

Finally, in verse 101 is the fifth and crowning reason. In a way, it is very similar to our second reason except the order is changed. Read the verse with me. What does David say he does in order to keep the Word? "I refrain my feet from every evil way." Verse 11 says that knowing God's Word will help you get back on to the right track. Verse 101 says I don't even select the wrong way now that the Word of God is a part of me. As you and I grow in our knowledge of the Bible, our choices should be affected. First, it will make clean what was dirty and eventually it will help us to stay on the right road. It will protect us and guide us on to the right path. You could call this *staying out of trouble*. It is one thing to say, "I was wrong, forgive me," and quite another to say, "No, I won't go there and do that, because it would injure my Lord."

Live It

Five reasons to memorize are recorded in Psalm 119. How many can you list (clean life, keep you from sin, wiser than enemies, more insight than teachers, stay out of trouble)?

Do you memorize? Do you work steadily at learning the commands of God? Will you learn a verse this week? I would suggest Psalm 119:9 and 11, and 98, 99 and 101. Come ready to recite at least one verse from memory next week. Watch your life to see the effect memorizing verses has on it.

To the Instructor: Make It Visual

Flashcards with arithmetic facts on them would be necessary for the opening. You will also need to prepare flashcards with each of the five reasons on them (*see examples on page 31*). Display them in a pocketboard or with tacks on a bulletin board. Have cards or slips of paper prepared for each pupil with one or more of the suggested verses to memorize on them. The best time to move them to action is *now*. Make it easier for them by distributing the verses on 3" x 5" cards. If a pupil claims to know these Scriptures, allow him to quote them to you and, upon successful completion, allow him to select another.

HOW CAN I MEMORIZE?

Scripture Text: *"And these words, which I command thee this day, shall be in thine heart" (Deut. 6:6).*

Lesson Aim: The student will be able to name three of the four "how-to's." The student will determine two "how-to's" to practice on a memory passage this week.

Are You Ready?

Our last lesson, from Psalm 119, gave reasons why we should memorize. How many of you did memorize a verse this week? (*Allow time for several to quote to the group the verse they learned. Others will benefit from hearing it quoted again and again.*) Thank you for your good work.

We said last time that it is easier to memorize something you really want to remember. There are several steps, though, between wanting to and actually learning verses. Today's lesson is a very practical lesson of "how-to."

Moses was ready to give his final words to the Children of Israel. They are recorded in Deuteronomy. Let's take a close look at Deuteronomy 6:6–9. He gives the parents helpful hints as to how they can teach their little ones the commands of the Lord. Open your Bible to see what they are.

See for Yourself

Now that you've found the place, let's read verses 6

33

through 9. What words in verse 6 tell you the topic here is memory? The words "shall be in thine heart" tell you the Lord wanted these commands to be a part of the people's working information. The first pointer is in verse 7. Tell us what it is. The parents were to *talk* of Scripture when they were sitting at home, when they went walking, when they went to bed and when they got up. Sounds like He really wanted them to get this. In that day if you weren't at home you would be out walking, the major method of travel. If you talked about something when you went to bed and when you got up, it would evidently be in your thoughts a lot.

The key here is to *read out loud.* Not only do you involve your thoughts, but your voice and your ears too. *If you want to learn a verse, read it out loud.* Psalm 119:99 uses the word "meditation." It means to reflect, to ponder, to talk with yourself aloud, to babble. In summary, to memorize, read out loud repeatedly.

Verses 8 and 9 give a second "how-to." Can you discover it? Tie them for a symbol on your hands and foreheads; write them on the doorframes of your houses and on your gates. *Write the verses in a number of places that you will see each day.* Write them on your hands as a reminder that they will guide all your hands do. Tie them like headbands to direct your thoughts. Display them on the front door and on the outer door for passersby to see. Write them, write them, write them!

A third "how-to" is to *say the verse to a friend, a parent, a sister or brother.* Verse 7 implies this by the encouragement to "teach them diligently." The parent is to teach and the child is to be taught. Two can learn so much more quickly than one alone. Whoever you have who will work with you is fine. Step three is to say it.

A fourth hint is implied here but stated more clearly in Isaiah 28:10. Listen as I read it to you, "For precept must be upon precept, precept upon precept; line upon line, . . . here a little, and there a little." The principle is to work a little a lot

34

of times. You can learn a phrase at a time, a line at a time, a thought at a time. The secret is that *you must do it again and again.*

Deuteronomy 6 says to do it at night, do it in the morning, do it while you are at home and while you are out. Time is important. Don't expect to learn what you are not willing to work on—it just will not happen. Here a little, there a little.

Live It

Now all of that is fine and good. It is easy to understand but hard to do. The best way to do it is to set up a plan and begin to do it. You know the four "how-to" steps we have discussed. They are (1) read it, (2) write it, (3) say it, (4) work a little a lot of times.

Please choose *two* of the "how-to" steps that you will use this week on one of the following verses. Next week you will have the opportunity to tell what you have learned.

Ecclesiastes 12:1	Psalm 1:1–3	John 20:31
1 Timothy 4:12	Psalm 19:1–2	1 John 1:7

(You may want to substitute verses, but the verses listed at the bottom of page 35 are suggestions if your group is not involved in steady memory work.)

To the Instructor: Make It Visual

A large wall mural would serve to list and diagram the steps discussed in this lesson. A roll of inexpensive shelf paper would serve the purpose for the mural. Crayons or felt markers will be fine for drawing. See the simple diagram on page 35 for ideas.

WHY CAN'T I MEMORIZE?

Scripture Text: *"The entrance of thy words giveth light; it giveth understanding unto the simple" (Ps. 119:130).*

Lesson Aim: The student will identify his reason for not memorizing Scripture. The student will determine to memorize a passage or verse that is new to him for the next class hour.

Are You Ready?

We have been talking about memorizing the Bible. The first week we explored the "why" of learning the Bible by memory. It has a multitude of positive effects on those who learn it.

Last time we met we talked about "how" to memorize. How many of the four steps can you remember? Which ones did you use in learning the verse for today? Please quote for us the verse you learned. (*Allow opportunity for students to respond. Their success will encourage them on to more work. Seeing friends doing memory work will be a positive motivator for those who are slower, shy or resistant. Make sure that you are doing what you ask them to do. They will do what they see you doing.*)

Today we will discuss some reasons why we don't memorize. Can you name some? (*As they do, write them down on a board for all to see.*) Those are good reasons; I have heard other students tell me the very same thing. Let's talk about some answers.

See for Yourself

"But I don't understand a word of this! How can I possibly learn it or ever memorize it when I don't have the faintest idea what it means?" This is a very common complaint and a fair one. It is not hard to memorize what you know and use often. But trying to memorize something from the Bible that is unfamiliar and difficult can give you double trouble. The answer is *not* to give up or refuse to learn, although many take this approach. How easily they are turned away from a good thing! Psalm 119:130 will give us some help at this point. Open your Bible to that place and read the verse. What gives us understanding? The entrance of God's Word gives light on the subject. In other words, in the process of memorizing we get understanding. As you repeat the verse and think on it over a period of time, you will understand. The word "entrance" means to open, to loosen, to carve, unstop. As the Bible gets into you it will make more sense. Ask a leader, your teacher or a parent for help. They have most likely been studying the Bible longer than you and they can help explain things to you.

"This is too long. I could never get this. Forget it! I don't even want to try. I would never get it all anyway." Sometimes it is true that adults ask too much of students. They forget just how much you can handle. There are other times, though, when the student gives up too easily. Do you remember how Isaiah 28:10 told us to memorize? You can learn it line upon line. Don't try to do all the work at once. A wise man said once, "Yard by yard, life's much too hard; but inch by inch, it's a cinch!"

"I'm such a poor student. I don't read well. School is torture to me. . . ." Check Proverbs 1:7, 8. What does it say about knowledge? We are told that the fear of the Lord is the beginning or starting place of knowledge. Do you ever consider that you may be a poor student because you don't memorize? It could be part of your difficulty. How will you fear the Lord if you don't know much about Him? By memorizing you will learn about Him—and be on your way to knowledge. The mental discipline of memorizing is great for sharpening your thoughts. As you concentrate on Scripture, you will find your mind sharper and clearer for other thinking. It's true . . . TRY IT!

"I really tried to memorize, but it was so boring I quit; well, I really never started. I just wasn't interested." If that's how you feel, you need to pay close attention to this next Scripture. It speaks straight to you. Open your Bible to 1 Corinthians 2:14. How does the natural man feel about the things of God? Two descriptions are given. He does not accept them. He feels they are foolish. Does that describe you? If it does, you are possibly a natural man. A man who is not a believer in the God of the Bible will have no use for God's Book. Your problem could be that you aren't a Christian. If that's true, you need to accept Christ as Savior. You won't be wanting to learn His Book until you yield to Him.

"I have absolutely no time to memorize. Every day I have school, cheerleading practice, play rehearsal, homework, chores to do at home, a part-time job and I try to sleep every night if I can." Does that sound ridiculous? Well, maybe, but it isn't far from the truth for many. Do you have time to be successful? Do you want your life to count for something? Read Joshua 1:8. Joshua tells us how to have a prosperous life. What does he say? The book of the law, the Bible, must be in our mouths. We should meditate on it; we should live it. Your life and mine will only be prosperous and successful when we *make* time to learn the Word. You will spend every minute of every day doing something. You decide what you do. If you want to be prosperous, memorize a little each day.

Live It

We have dealt with five reasons why pupils don't

memorize. Let me rehearse them for you. As I do, evaluate your reasons. Which of them are you using?

> (1) I don't understand . . .
> (2) It's too long . . .
> (3) I'm not a good student . . .
> (4) I'm really not interested . . .
> (5) I don't have time . . .

Now consider the answers. Will you choose to memorize?

> If you don't understand, then ask for someone to explain.
>
> If it's too long, do your work one line at a time.
>
> If you're not a good student, memorize and you'll progress in school.
>
> If you are not interested, determine whether you know Christ as Savior. If not, receive Him today!
>
> If you don't have time, make time.

Before you leave today, select a passage to learn for next week. I would suggest: Psalm 119:130; Proverbs 1:7, 8; Joshua 1:8; Isaiah 28:10; 1 Corinthians 2:14.

To the Instructor: Make It Visual

Teacher, are you allowing your students to answer questions? You should be. They need to be personally involved in reading the verses and thinking out the answers. Following each question in the lesson text, you need to allow time for finding references and for answering. An answer is given so that you might be prepared to keep on the right track. Encourage your learners to be active by allowing them to think and respond.

You may desire to role play the excuses of non-memorizers. Be dramatic and exaggerate; it will make your point more recognizable. It would be fun for the students to tape record the excuses ahead of time. Use different voices for each excuse. Play it to the group and watch their interest. For the final section, do have the excuses and answers written for all to see. You may decide to use the overhead, the chalkboard, a pocketboard, a make-it-yourself slide or prewritten strips to be displayed on a flannelboard or bulletin board. Below are some visual suggestions.

Ready to
Grow?

BEFORE GOD SAVED ME

Scripture Text: *"That at that time ye were without Christ, being aliens . . . and strangers . . . having no hope, and without God in the world" (Eph. 2:12).*

Lesson Aim: The student will be able to name and explain simply four terms that the Bible uses to describe those not in the family of God.

Are You Ready?

We will begin an important set of studies together. These are things that all of us need to know. No matter who you are or what you believe about yourself and God, these are for you. We will be using our Bibles a lot. It is good for you to learn how to look up verses in the Bible, to read them and to be able to understand what they say.

Today's lesson is about *before.* The Bible has a lot to say about all men and their condition and relationship to God *before* they are saved from sin. We will look at eight verses. In each one, read to find what it says about an individual who has not yet come to God for salvation.

See for Yourself

We begin today in the Old Testament book of Isaiah. Open your Bible to Isaiah 53:6. What animal does it say we are like? We are like sheep. What have we done? Each one of us has left the right path or "gone astray" as Isaiah puts it. We are each going our own way, not God's way. Sheep are quite stubborn and not too smart. They often wander from the path of safety, getting into trouble. We, like sheep, are off the path God has for us. How many are included in this description? ALL—none may escape.

Next, open your Bible to Romans 5:6. What does this verse tell you about our condition? We were without strength; we were ungodly. Have you ever been very sick? When you started to recover, you were feeling better but still very weak. You were powerless and maybe even helpless. There wasn't much that you could defend yourself against. God did *not* die for you and me because we were strong. The word "ungodly" means sinful, wicked. We were weak in our sin.

Check Romans 5:10 to see how we are described. If you read carefully you will find that before we are saved, we are enemies of God. An enemy hates another and wishes to injure him. How do you treat an enemy? You make fun, call him names, try to hurt him. Before we are saved we also treat God as an enemy. As His enemy we have no desire to be near Him or those who love Him.

Ephesians 2:1 is our next Scripture clue. What do you see there? What does it say we were? Yes, we were dead in trespasses and sins. To be dead is to be powerless. Dead people can't act; they are not able to talk, to work, to do anything. That's how we are before we come to God. Some people think they can do something to please God. They forget that they are dead spiritually.

John 3:18 sounds like a courtroom with a judge and a jury. What we were is described as "those that believe not." What is the word? Condemned! What does it mean? We are guilty of wrongdoing and will be punished accordingly. If you don't believe on the Lord Jesus you are condemned already. You don't have to wait until a future time—the verdict has already been given. You are guilty and ready for God's sentence on you.

46

Let's review for a moment. Can you recall the words that describe us before we come to Christ for salvation? If you say we are like sheep who have wandered from the path, without strength, enemies of God, dead in sin and condemned you are exactly right. That paints a very hopeless picture. There are three more passages to consider today before we draw some conclusions.

John 3:36 tells what the sentence is for the condemned ones. Read it to yourself and be ready to tell the group. What did you find? He that believeth not the Son shall not see life. Furthermore, God's wrath or anger continues on him. This is a hard penalty in two parts. He that is without Christ is not permitted to have eternal life. Since life is in God's Son and this person is an enemy of God, it is reasonable that he would be denied extended time in the presence of his enemy. The Bible book of Revelation describes the wrath of God as it is unloosed in a future time. God's horrible wrath is directed at those who continue to oppose Him.

The last two descriptions are found together in Ephesians 2:12, 13. (*Insist that your students read and give you the proper answers. They would prefer to guess but this is of no value in their learning. Encourage them to read and respond—not to guess.*) Notice the past tense—we *were*. What were we? We were without Christ, aliens, strangers, hopeless. One little girl when reading this verse said, "I feel like you drew a circle and I was left out." That is true, except that God drew the circle, not her teacher. If you don't belong to Christ, you are without Him. You are like an alien who belongs to another country. That fact may cause you to feel strange, but the saddest part is the last. You have no hope. There is no possibility for your situation to get any better.

Check verse 13. In Christ we are near, but without Him we are far off. All of us like to be near. We have a natural fear of being cut off.

Live It

This lesson is depressing. It paints a truthful picture of us

47

and our position without Christ. If you are a believer, you should rejoice in all you have escaped. By God's great kindness you are His child and have been released from sin's power.

If you are without Christ, you need to realistically look at what the Bible says about your present and future condition. You may feel very safe right now, but remember what the truth is about your present condition. You may think you are on the right track. Proverbs 14:12 says, "There is a way which seemeth right unto a man, but the end thereof are the ways of death." Receive Christ today and you will no longer be:

    A. A wandering sheep
    B. Without strength, ungodly
    C. The enemy of God
    D. Dead in sin
    E. Condemned
    F. Under wrath
    G. An alien, stranger, with no hope
    H. Far from God

Acts 16:31 puts it so clearly, ". . . Believe on the Lord Jesus Christ, and thou shalt be saved. . . ."

As we begin our series on growing we each need to take notice of where we are. If you are already in Christ, proceed to lesson two, giving thanks for your salvation. If you don't know Christ, receive Him today!

To the Instructor: Make It Visual

The students will enjoy making their own visuals of each of the verses you have studied in this lesson. Provide paper, markers, crayons and supervision. Allow them time but set a limit—they will use whatever you allow. Meet back together and share what was drawn. Much more will be retained if the students are able to get involved actively in the learning process. Display their work for all to see. Some ideas are given on the following page. The transfer of ideas from words to pictures is critical in understanding and internalizing that what they read refers to them and not to someone somewhere else.

49

YOU ARE IN CHRIST

Scripture Text: *"But as many as received him, to them gave he power to become the sons of God, even to them that believe on his name" (John 1:12).*

Lesson Aim: The student will be able to list three of the five descriptions that are true of those in Christ.

Are You Ready?

Have you ever moved to a new town to live? As you rode along the highway you may have crossed a state border. At the entrance you saw a sign that said, "Welcome to _____. You are now in the state of _____ ." Farther along another sign informed you that you were entering a certain county. And still later you saw a sign welcoming you to the city that would be your home. As you made the journey you knew where you were. You knew what state, country and city you were in.

There were many details about your new home, however, that you didn't know until you'd lived there for a while. As you discovered them they became important to you.

Today's lesson is similar to moving to a new town. You are aware that you are a Christian. You know that a definite change has taken place but you don't know all the details yet. We will explore five important changes that happened to you when you came to Christ. They are true whether you know about them or not. But you can only enjoy them as you are aware of them.

See for Yourself

I love to explore. How about you? Our map will be the New Testament.

Clue #1 is recorded for you to find in 1 Corinthians 11:1. What does Paul say he was? A follower of Christ. What are we to do? We are to follow Paul as he followed Christ. If we follow carefully, Who will we really be following? Yes, Christ will be our Leader. The word "follow" here means to go after in order to catch. You get the idea that there is a desire to arrive at the same place. Our last lesson said we were like stray sheep before we came to Christ. What a change—once we wandered away, now we follow!

Clue #2 is in John's Gospel, John 1:12. We were the enemies of God, ready to oppose Him and do Him injury. Now what are we? We are given power and authority to be His sons! Sons have access to their fathers. A son is cared for, loved, provided for and made an heir of what the father owns. That is remarkable—to be changed from God's enemy to His son. And, remember, we were dead; so none of the credit goes to us. God is totally responsible for our new status.

We were dead in sins but Clue #3, in John 3:16, tells of our new situation. Read it and tell us what you see there. God gave His Son so that those believing should not perish or die, but exchange their death for life that lasts forever. Again we see God and His Son at work, providing for everyone life that will never end. It is life that always goes on. Are you alive or dead?

Please open your Bible to Colossians 1:14. Here we find Clue #4. This is a letter to the members of a church in the Bible town of Colosse. Paul is writing to them and he is remembering Who God the Father is and all that He has done. Verse 14 is in the middle of his thoughts. The word "whom" refers to God. What do the Colossian believers and Paul, and

51

you and I, if we know Him as Savior, have? We have forgiveness of sins. "Forgiven" means to pardon, to stop being angry with. In our last lesson we discussed that we were condemned. We are guilty sinners, but through Christ's death our sins are taken away. Christ was crucified in your place and mine. My sins are forgiven. God did not overlook my sins, but I was dead and couldn't do anything about them myself. Christ died for me. He was condemned and I go free.

Finally, Clue #5 is a contrast to our former condition as aliens, strangers, being far off. Ephesians 1:6 says, ". . . wherein he hath made us accepted in the beloved." Doesn't that sound good? In Christ we are no longer outsiders, aliens. We are accepted not for who we are or what we can offer, but because we are in Him. There is a gospel song that says, "In the beloved, accepted am I . . . for in the person of God's Son I am as dear as He." What a good place to be. Ephesians 2:13 completes our thoughts with these words, "*But* now in Christ Jesus ye who sometimes were far off are made nigh by the blood of Christ."

Live It

How about you today? Are you a follower of Christ or a sheep wanting to go your own way? If you follow Christ you will inherit Heaven. Go your own way and you'll have destruction and separation.

Are you God's son or His avowed enemy? Are you against Him or with Him? The hymnwriter asks the question, "Who Is on the Lord's Side?" No one knows better than you. You may become His son by believing on Him and receiving His death as payment for your sin.

Do you have eternal life or are you dead in your sin? You need not remain dead. God's gift is for you.

Are you still far off? Do you feel uncomfortable, strange during the Bible story time? That could be an indication that you are not yet "accepted in the beloved."

If you are new in Christ—rejoice today! You are a

follower, His son. You have eternal life; you are forgiven; you are accepted! Live like it!

To the Instructor: Make It Visual

The pictures that the students drew for last week will be necessary for today's work. Make sure that they are displayed at eye level to the pupils and in the order that they will be referred to today.

A chart is necessary to visualize the contrast of the last session and today's lesson. A sample follows. You may use an overhead which you prepare ahead and reveal one line at a time, or use the chalkboard and add as you go along. The finished chart should be similar to this.

BEFORE SALVATION	IN CHRIST
Stray Sheep	Follower of Christ
Enemy	Son of God
Dead	Life forever
Condemned	Forgiven
Alien, far off	Accepted, near Him

IDENTIFIED WITH CHRIST

Scripture Text: *"Buried with him in baptism, wherein also ye are risen with him through the faith . . ." (Col. 2:12).*

Lesson Aim: The student will be able to explain the meaning of baptism as identification with Christ. The student will be able to give the Biblical order of salvation before baptism.

Are You Ready?

In what branch of the military are these men? How do you know? (*Display picture of a soldier in Army greens, a sailor in dress white and a pilot in uniform.*) What is the occupation of these individuals? How do you know? (*Show magazine photos of a nurse, a policeman and a basketball player.*) You were able to tell me what these people do because their uniforms identified them.

To be identified with a job is accomplished partly by wearing a uniform. There are other ways to identify an individual, but his clothing is easy for all to see. To identify employees of a company because of a uniform means to connect them as having something in common. They dress alike because their work is alike.

Some religious groups wear uniforms. They are easily identified because of their clothing. Today we will discuss being identified as a follower of Christ. As Christians we don't

54

wear special uniforms, but we do have a special way to identify ourselves with Christ. We will talk about baptism. What does baptism mean, how are we baptized, why are we baptized and, finally, when should we be baptized?

See for Yourself

Baptism is described in Colossians 2:12. Open your Bible to that place and read along with me. Baptism is a testimony to all who watch that the one baptized belongs to Christ. It is a picture to those who observe that a change of heart has already taken place inside. Baptism is outward and easy to see. It is a visible way to tell others that your sins are *already* forgiven and you are on your way to Heaven. Some people are saved but do not want to be baptized. They do not want others to know that they belong to Christ. This is not right; we will talk more about it later.

Colossians 2:12 says that we do two things with Him (with Christ) in the action of baptism. What are they? First, we are *buried* with Him. Second, we are *risen* with Him. The first pictures Christ's death for sin on the cross, then His burial. The second pictures Christ's resurrection, His return to life, His rising from the dead. I did not die on a cross; Christ died for me. He died, He was buried, He came back to life. When I am baptized, I identify with Him by standing, being "buried" in the water and coming up out of the water. Baptism is an outward symbol or picture of an inward change.

Listen carefully as three verses are read aloud to discover the details of *how* baptism was performed in the Bible. (*Assign good readers to read Matthew 3:16, John 3:22, 23 and Acts 8:38.*) What information did you gather? (*Take time after each reference lest they be confused or forgotten.*) Jesus went up out of the water. If He came up out of the water, He must have been down in the water. John had chosen his place for baptizing because there was *much* water there. Philip baptized the man in Acts by taking him down *into* the water. The word "baptize" means to dip, to plunge, to submerge. That makes

55

sense when you realize that it is a picture of Christ's burial. When a grave is closed it is covered with dirt, not sprinkled or partially covered. To be an accurate picture the individual must be immersed—completely covered with water.

As Jesus was leaving earth He gave final instructions to His disciples. They were to spend their lives doing what Matthew 28:18–20 says. Listen as I read it to you. "Go ye therefore, and teach all nations, baptizing them in the name of the Father, and of the Son, and of the Holy Ghost. . . ." As they were going they were to teach and baptize. Jesus felt that baptism was important. As we are taught and come to salvation, we, too, should be baptized. Why? We should because He instructed the disciples to do this in all nations until the end of the world. That includes you and me. John 14:15 says that if we love the Lord, we will keep His commands. We are also told to follow Him, and part of His path was His own baptism by John.

The last question is very important. It asks, "When should I be baptized?" The actual date or time cannot be learned from the Bible but an order of events is given. Read the example of Lydia in Acts 16:14 and 15. What was the order? She heard Paul. Her heart was opened. She responded to what she heard. She was baptized. In the same chapter, verses 32 through 33, the order is similar. The jailer heard, he responded in belief, he was baptized. Later in Acts 18:8 we read, "And Crispus . . . believed on the Lord with all his house; and . . . were baptized." Belief *must* come first! If it does not, baptism cannot identify you with Christ. The water will make you wet; it cannot change your heart.

Live It

How about you? Do you know Christ? Have you heard of His death for you? Have you believed? If you say yes, then you are ready to be baptized. Speak to your pastor this week and tell him of your desire. He will work with you.

If you answered no, then you are not ready for baptism.

Your need is to receive Christ. You need a change of heart. Receive Him today.

To the Instructor: Make It Visual

For the opening session you will need pictures of men in military uniform, plus magazine pictures of a nurse, policeman and basketball player. A prepared teacher continually collects and files pictures so that they are ready for use when needed. If you don't have a picture file, begin one today. Use old magazines and other advertising materials, catalogs, etc.

Bring a basin and an object to class. Fill the basin with water and demonstrate the meaning of the word "baptize." Demonstrate why other methods do not satisfy the definition.

It would be helpful to draw the three positions of baptism as described in Colossians 2:12 and label each. A suggested idea is given here.

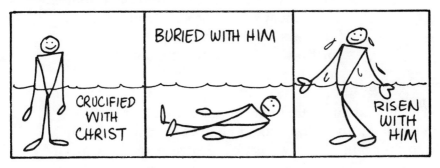

THE LORD'S TABLE FOR YOU?

Scripture Text: *"For I have received of the Lord that which also I delivered unto you, That the Lord Jesus the same night in which he was betrayed took bread" (1 Cor. 11:23).*

Lesson Aim: The student will be able to describe the food and drink used and tell what they symbolize. The student should be able to explain who (believers only) and when (often till He comes) we celebrate this memory meal.

Are You Ready?

Eating is an important part of our daily activities. We begin the day with food, break at noon to eat and gather at night to eat again. Often we snack in between and have a bed-time snack. Eating is a fun activity for most children and adults.

The Jews in the Bible had many occasions that included eating a special meal. One of their special meals was called the Passover. It was a reminder that their God had secured their release from Pharaoh and Egypt. Each year after they left Egypt, they were to eat bread without yeast (unleavened bread) and a roast lamb to celebrate this important event.

Today we celebrate a meal in our church services that is similar to the Passover meal. We call it the Lord's Table because the Lord Jesus conducted the very first meal like it. In fact, the very night that Jesus died He took time to instruct His disciples about this meal and what it meant. The question we hope to answer today is what the Lord's Table means to you and me.

See for Yourself

Today we will be studying 1 Corinthians 11:23–30. Please open your Bible to that place and read these verses out loud with me.

These verses explain many of the details of Jesus' special meal with His disciples. Paul tells us that he heard this from the Lord and was giving it to these Corinthian Christians so that they would hold similar meals. He gave it to them just like he heard it.

What food was used in this special meal? Check verse 23. They used bread. In other places in the Bible we discover that the bread was unleavened or made without yeast, which would make it rise. The reason is because leaven is a picture of sin in the Bible. This bread was to be a symbol of Someone very important Who was perfect. Read verse 24 and tell us of Whom the bread was a symbol. Jesus said it was a picture of Him and of His body. What did Jesus do with the bread (v. 24 again)? He broke it and gave it to the disciples to eat. It was a picture of Jesus' death, when His body would be broken. Now do you understand why the bread was to have no leaven? Jesus was perfect—without sin. What else was used in the special meal? Check verse 25. It says Jesus took the cup and drank from it. From Luke 22:18 we learn that it contained juice from grapes. This was a symbol of what? It pictured the blood of Jesus. It was necessary for His blood to be given to cover the penalty for sin.

Who took part in the first Lord's Supper? In verse 24 Jesus says, ". . . this is my body, which is broken for *you*. . . ." Who was He talking to? The twelve disciples. They were His followers, His closest friends, men who believed Jesus to be God's Son. So we know that the disciples and Jesus took part.

59

Paul wrote to the Corinthian Christians about this event so they too could take part. Following this pattern, we understand that the Lord's Table is for Christians, true followers of Christ.

When was this first meal held? Read 11:23 carefully. It was held the same night in which Jesus was betrayed by Judas. It must have been important for Jesus to use His last few hours to teach these men what this meal meant and how they were to prepare it. Jesus made a request for the disciples to continue holding meals like this. How often were they to do that? Look at verse 26. That night Jesus was betrayed and within hours He was crucified. They were to begin at His death and continue to do it *often* until He came again. Churches have different schedules for holding this meal. Many do it once a month, some more often, some less often, some on special occasions to recall the Lord's death. It is not optional—verse 25 says *this do*! We are told to continue doing it until Jesus comes.

The most important part of this lesson is the next part. It asks "Why?" Why celebrate the Lord's Supper? Why did Jesus ask us to? What should be our attitude?

The final phrase of verse 24 says they were to be doing this "in remembrance of me"—to remember Jesus. Again at the end of verse 25, Jesus repeats, "this do . . . in remembrance of me." Verse 26 adds a little more. In holding this meal we proclaim the Lord's death till He come. We tell others about our Lord's death by observing and entering into this meal. We are not to think about the food (v. 34) but about the Lord and His death. Jesus said this is the new testament or the new agreement. The old agreement called for sacrificing animals and giving their blood to *cover* sin. Jesus proclaims the old agreement is *over*!!! This is the new agreement. Once His blood was given, there was no longer any need for animal blood. The followers of Jesus were to drink juice as a reminder that they need not kill any more animals.

Let's review. What was used in this meal? Bread and juice from grapes. Who is to eat it? The disciples, the Corinthians, all believers in Christ. When should we do it? Often, from His death till He comes. Why should we do it? To remember Jesus' death, to celebrate the new agreement and to tell others of His death for us!

Live It

We can know all the facts and still not participate properly. Paul records a strong warning in 11:27, 28. What is the warning? If we take part in an unworthy manner, we are guilty of the body and blood of the Lord.

The point is not that you are to be worthy of taking part. In ourselves we could never be worthy of Christ's death for us. Paul is talking about our attitude and actions at the Lord's Table.

Several Corinthians took part unworthily. They brought judgment on themselves from God in the form of sickness and weakness and many even died! They misunderstood the purpose of this table and made it a feasting, overeating time. Our attention should be on our Lord's death, not on the food.

You and I need to be aware of the purpose of this table. It is for believers only! If you are not a Christian do not take part, for you will stir God's anger and receive His judgment. Focus your attention on His death for you. As a Christian, give thanks and tell Him of your love. You will want to be quietly praying and thinking, not laughing or making commotion. Do it *often* till Jesus comes.

To the Instructor: Make It Visual

A teaching picture of the Passover will help establish the historical backdrop of today's study. Point out the various foods involved in that meal. Also have available a flannelgraph or teaching picture of the Last Supper. As each point is made, point out each item in the picture. Many students have seen a picture of the Last Supper but have little or no idea of its meaning. Use this teaching moment to advantage.

Cut signs for the major points of the Bible search from

large cardboard or construction paper: What? Who? When? Why? Warning!!

Below is a simple drawing that could be used to illustrate several of the points of the lesson.

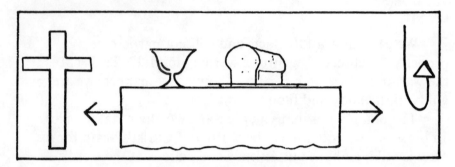

If possible, invite a deacon or your pastor in to show the elements and equipment used in serving the Lord's Table. Give the instruction first and then allow time for questions and answers.

GOD'S CHURCH IN MY TOWN

Scripture Text: *"And he [Christ] is the head of the body, the church . . . (Col. 1:18).*

Lesson Aim: The student will be able to define the church as the Body of Christ, the "called out ones." The student will evaluate whether he is a member of the true church.

Are You Ready?

Today we will study some of what the New Testament has to say about the word "church." The word "church" is used in different ways to mean different things. What meanings do you know for this word? (*Allow a time for discussion. There will be a variety of responses. All are acceptable because they indicate what the pupils understand about the topic at hand. Listen carefully to what they say, not to what you want them to say.*)

We refer to the building where people meet to have religious services as a church. All the people in a particular denomination call themselves the church. The group or individual groups of a particular denomination form the _____ Church U.S.A. or the _____ Church International.

The English word "church" is found 114 times in the Bible's New Testament. Ninety-one of these references speak of the church in a specific geographic location. Let's take a closer look.

63

See for Yourself

We will talk about the following: What is the Bible idea of the church? Who began it and when was it first conceived? When did it begin? When will it officially be completed?

Open your Bible to Colossians 1:18. This verse describes the Lord Jesus. It refers to Christ as "he." What does this verse call the church? It is a Body. The Head of that Body is Christ. A body is an organism that is alive; it has many members or parts. Likewise, the Church is alive and has many people in it. What does your head do for your body? It gives directions, makes decisions, begins action and so on. In the same way, the Lord Jesus gives direction to His Church. He should be the source of all action and decisions. Often we like to pick a person to be the head. This is a function that belongs to Christ alone.

The first two verses of Colossians tell who was in the Colossian group. Can you name them? The saints and faithful brethren in Christ who were at Colosse made up the Colossian church. They were all *in* Christ, they had believed Him and received Him as their Lord and Savior. They were all in the same town and so they joined together with Christ as their Head to form the church at Colosse. Similar groups were formed in Rome, Corinth, Philippi, Thessalonica, Ephesus and Crete. Simply said, a church is a group of "called out ones," people who are called out of the world and allegiance to Satan, to love and work for the true God. The word for church means just that—the "called out ones."

So, the Bible idea of church has nothing to do with the building where the church meets. It doesn't refer to man-made organizations that are called churches. A true church has only those who know Christ as Savior.

Who first thought of calling out people to make churches in different towns? Read Ephesians 1:3, 4 for the answer.

God was the Originator of the Chruch. He did so before He even began to create Adam, Eve and the world. This verse tells us that God even had specific people in mind when He

64

laid those plans. The Church was certainly *not* an afterthought.

The first time the word "church" appears in the Bible is in Matthew's Gospel. Through all of the Old Testament's two thousand plus years, God was silent about His plan to build His Church. Jesus began to slowly reveal the plan in the New Testament. By a careful search through the New Testament, it is possible to establish Acts 2 as the birthday of this plan that God had in mind since eternity past.

Following the birth of the Church, you find repeated references to the Church. Acts 2:41 and 2:47 are examples. Who was added to the church? Those who received Peter's message and were baptized. Who did the adding? The Lord added daily all who were saved.

All during the present time the Lord is calling out a people for the Body, His Church. When the Body is complete, Ephesians 5:27 tells you what He intends to do with her. What is that? He will present her to Himself. She will be glorious, having no spot or imperfection or wrinkle. Second Thessalonians 2:1 describes that event as the coming of our Lord Jesus Christ and His gathering together of His Body. We call that event the Rapture.

Live It

All that we have discussed today may be new to you. The important question is whether you are part of Christ's Church. Are you one of His called out ones or are you still in Satan's crowd? By believing the true message of Christ's death, burial and resurrection you may also be in His Church. If you are saved, have you been baptized and joined God's "called out ones" in your town? In Acts, people were saved, baptized and added to the Church regularly. They were anxious to be identified with Christ and other believers. If you are ready to join your local church, speak to your pastor this week and tell him of your interest. He will help you to do what is necessary. Follow the pattern in Acts 2:41: "Then they that gladly received his word were baptized: and the same day there were added unto them about three thousand souls."

To the Instructor: Make It Visual

Display a number of magazine pictures of churches around the teaching area. You may also find old bulletin covers and teaching pictures helpful.

Bring some sort of toy or doll to class to demonstrate the relationship of a head to a body. It is much easier to comprehend if you visualize it.

The following drawing is a capsule summary of the major points of the lesson. You may duplicate it on a poster, an overhead, chalkboard, or even a bulletin board or flannelboard. A time line is also included for the clarification of the sequence of events.

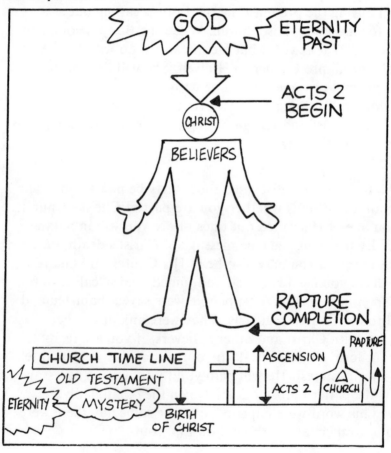

AM I SAFE IN JESUS?

Scripture Text: *"And I give unto them eternal life; and they shall never perish, neither shall any man pluck them out of my hand" (John 10:28).*

Lesson Aim: The student will be able to explain why salvation is sure, giving some of these reasons: Christ promised it; the Father provides it; God's power guarantees it. The student will be encouraged to evaluate his own reaction to the truth of being secure in Christ.

Are You Ready?

Please review these pictures carefully. (*You will need to display three or four magazine pictures that feature hands. The individual who belongs to the hands should not be shown. The pictures should show the hands involved in different activities.*) What do these pictures have that is the same? Yes, each one shows a hand. They are doing different things, but they are all hands.

Describe the person these hands might belong to. (*Allow interaction. Several should be encouraged to share their thoughts. This is a "safe question" which all can answer. The answer is right because the one responding is telling what he thinks. These sorts of questions are excellent to begin a lesson because many may respond.*)

If you were in trouble or lost, which of these hands would you rather be held by? Why?

How do you feel when you walk with a man with a strong, loving hand on yours? I feel safe, confident that he can handle the hard things ahead of us. Today we will discover what it means to be held in God's hand. Jesus talked about this in John 10.

See for Yourself

Open your Bible to John 10:22. Listen and follow along as I read through verse 25. Where was Jesus? Verse 22 tells us that He was at Jerusalem. Who came to Him at Solomon's porch to ask a question? The Jews circled around Jesus and asked a really tricky question. They were trying to trip Jesus up, placing blame on Him for their unbelief. Jesus didn't allow them to get away with this.

What did they want to know? They had asked, "Who are you?" The reply came, "I have already told you and you did not believe."

In verse 26 Jesus declares that there is a big difference between the unbelieving Jews and the true followers. Listen to His description of His sheep in verses 27–30. "My sheep hear my voice, and I know them, and they follow me: And I give unto them eternal life; and they shall never perish, neither shall any man pluck them out of my hand. My Father, which gave them me, is greater than all; and no man is able to pluck them out of my Father's hand."

What kind of life do the followers of Christ have? Verse 28 calls it eternal life. What does "eternal" mean? Eternal means always going on and never stopping. Eternal life goes on and on and on and on. Who gives this never-ending life? Jesus does. Does He change His mind, get hurt and want it back? No, that is not how He is. He is true to His word.

When will those who have this eternal life perish? Silly question? Well it may sound so to you, but some children, young people and adults doubt God's Word. They believe that once they have this eternal life they can still perish.

In Whose hand are those that follow Christ, according to verse 28? We are in Jesus' hand. Are we safe there? Can an enemy or anyone get us away from Him? Why do you say that? Yes, we are safe. No enemy, not even Satan or any of his demons, can steal us out of our place of safety.

Listen carefully and read verse 29 aloud with me. If all of verses 27 and 28 don't make you feel safe in Christ, verse 29 surely should. How is the Father described here? He is greater than *all*. What do you suppose God's hand would be like? It would be strong and safe and secure. We know that God doesn't have actual hands because that would limit Him. But by talking as if God had hands we can picture how safe we are. We know from verse 29 that God is safely keeping all who are His.

How many reasons have we covered today that make Christians sure they are safe in Christ? Name as many as you can. (1) We have *eternal* life. (2) We will *never* perish. (3) Jesus promised us. (4) We are in Jesus' hand. (5) We are in God's hand. (6) God is more powerful than anyone else.

Live It

What about you? Are you like the Jews who didn't believe Jesus? They wanted to stone Him to death when He talked of being sure about belonging to God. They were full of unbelief. Do you belong to Christ? Are you His follower?

If you are a believer, a follower of Jesus, you should feel safe and glad about all that we have read today. All of those reasons that a believer is safe in Christ are true for and about you today. You already have ETERNAL LIFE; you will never perish; Jesus will securely keep you in His hand; you are in God's powerful protection. Rest in His promise, His protection and His powerful hands. You are safe in Him.

The man named Paul in the Bible was a real enemy of God at first, and He hated God and killed Christians faithfully. He was a wicked man, yet when he came to Christ he was forgiven. In 2 Timothy 1:12 he says, ". . . I know whom

I have believed [that is Jesus], and am persuaded that he [Jesus] is able to keep that which I have committed unto him. . . ." The word "keep" means to guard my deposit. Paul felt very safe in Christ. He was as safe as God was strong.

How about you? Are you in His hand today? You can be, you know.

To the Instructor: Make It Visual

As was already explained, you will need pictures of several hands doing different activities. Select one of a strong, rugged man's hand. Don't forget to use your own hands as a visual aid to demonstrate God's care for the believer. Explain to the students that every time they look at their own hands, they can be reminded of the care and safety of being in the Lord's hand.

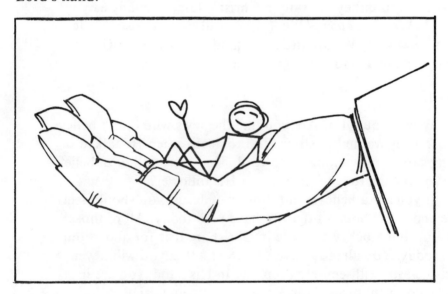

SET ASIDE FOR GOD

Scripture Text: *"Love not the world, neither the things that are in the world. If any man love the world, the love of the Father is not in him" (1 John 2:15).*

Lesson Aim: The student will be able to define separation as set aside for a special purpose. Given the use of the Bible and the references (2 John 10, 11; Rom. 16:17, 20; 2 Cor. 6:16, 17; 1 John 2:15, 17), he should give the reasons *why* he should stay away from false teachers, troublemakers, unclean things, the world system.

Are You Ready?

For a moment, talk to me about Christians. Is it important who they select for their closest friends? Yes or no and why? All of us need friends. Friends are important to life. Each of us needs to have people we are close to, to spend time with, to do things with. Do God's people have to be different from everyone else? Can we do anything and everything that our unsaved friends do? Why or why not?

Today we want to talk about something that is hard to do. It is hard because it affects how we live, who we are with, what we do, why we do or don't do certain things. The official word is "separation." Many Christian people feel really angry

71

and hot about what this means to them. Most discussions about separation are full of "no's" and "do not's." While that is helpful, we want to talk mostly about "why."

See for Yourself

We will discuss three reasons why Christians should be set apart from the world for God's use. You will need your Bible and a ready heart. As we study, evaluate your friends and activities against these reasons. God will show you what He wants you to do if you are open to Him and His way. Ready?

First, open your Bible to the New Testament book of 1 Corinthians. It follows the book of Romans. We will take a closer look at 1 Corinthians 6:19, 20. Remember, this book was written to church members. Paul called them saints—set apart ones in Christ Jesus (1:2). Who did Paul tell them they belonged to? They belonged to God. How did they know they belonged to God? Their body was the place where the Holy Spirit lived. Their "housemate" was a gift from God. They were bought with a price. What was the price paid by God to buy us from Satan and sin? God gave His Son Who came to earth and died a cruel death to buy us. When you buy something at the store with your own money, who decides how it is used? Why you, of course! It is your purchase, so you have every reason to use what you have paid for. Since we are God's purchased possession, does He have a right to determine our choice of friends and activities? Remember, as your "housemate" the Holy Spirit has to go wherever you take your body. He has no choice, but *you* do. You rightfully belong to the Father. You are to be set apart for God because you always represent Him.

Second, open your Bible to 1 Peter 1:15, 16. Read what you find there. You may want to exchange the word "conversation" for "manner of life." Who called Christians? God did, in Christ Jesus. What is He like, this One Who called us? He is holy, pure, without sin or error, perfect! What are we to be? Holy in all our manner of life. That doesn't leave any areas out, does it? No, it covers all the bases. Why are we to be holy? First, because it is written down. We can't claim we didn't know. God wrote it down in both the Old and New Testaments. Second, we are to be pure and clean in life because we are called out by a holy God. We carry the family name and so must act in a way that honors His name and character.

Third, there are specific people or groups of people that the Christian will stay away from. Not only are we told who to avoid, but *why*. Below are four references and four groups to separate from. Use your Bible and complete the chart.

WHO?		WHY?
	2 John 10, 11	
	Romans 16:17, 20	
	2 Corinthians 6:16, 17	
	1 John 2:15, 17	

Second John tells us to not invite false teachers into our houses, nor to greet them. If you do invite them in or give them blessing, you are taking part in their evil work. Romans 16 says to mark those who cause divisions and offenses contrary to the true teaching you have learned. They are troublemakers—avoid them. They don't serve Christ but themselves, and they deceive hearts. Second Corinthians talks of coming out from unbelievers, idol-worshipers and the unclean ones.

The reason we don't associate with these people is that we don't have agreement with them. We are of opposing beliefs. By being removed from them, what is true in the heart becomes open to the eye.

Finally, 1 John says stay away from the world and the world's things. Why do we not love them? They have an end that we don't! Why get attached when we will have to give it up? As Christians, we belong to an eternal system.

Live It

Make a mental list of your closest friends. Are they false teachers, troublemakers, unclean, lovers of the world? If they are and you hang on to them, you, too, will slowly but surely become confused about what you believe. You will be drawn away from serving Christ and will serve yourself, and may even become a reason for others to doubt Christ. Do you really agree with their unbelief? Their unbelief *cannot* make you a stronger Christian; it will only weaken you. As you love them you will get attached to the world system they love and hang on to it, too. All they have in life is the world and its things. You have Christ, eternity, life, forgiveness, freedom!

You belong to God because He has purchased you. He wants you to live up to the family name "Christ-ian," a Christ-one. As a believer you are set apart, not to make you miserable, but to make you strong in faith, vibrant in serving God and free to draw others to the eternal benefits in Christ. Separation is not missing out, dropping out, losing out. It is God's loving way of protecting you and keeping you useful to others. Be set apart for God! Others will see your life and be drawn to Christ. The choice is yours! Make your decision permanent with the Lord, in prayer, right now.

To the Instructor: Make It Visual

One way to begin the lesson is to write the word "separation" on the board. Ask for volunteers to pronounce it and define it. A role play of two students who have the wrong attitude and reaction to separation would be effective. Really overact to establish the point. This will help lead into a discussion of friends and activities.

Prepare a chart for the final Bible search activity. See page 73 for details. You may either prepare a large one for all to see or an individual sheet for each student. The more involved the student becomes in study and response the better his learning. Saturate your lesson in prayer. The enemy will be working overtime to distract and confuse.

IS IT RIGHT OR WRONG?

Scripture Text: *"Whether therefore ye eat, or drink, or whatsoever ye do, do all to the glory of God" (1 Cor. 10:31).*

Lesson Aim: The student will be able to recite three of the four guidelines for choosing the acceptable and right activities for a Christian.

Are You Ready?

"Mom, can I go with Jeff to. . . ." This question comes up very often in the homes of older children and young teens. Still under the responsibility of Mom and Dad, the young person must request permission and money to go to an activity with a friend.

Life has many responsibilities and choices. When we are young our parents, teachers and other adults help us or make most of our decisions for us. As we grow older, we are free to make more of our own decisions. With the freedom to choose comes the need to know how to make wise decisions.

Some activities are easy to make decisions about. They are plainly wrong, sinful, and declared so in the Bible, or they are good, positive, healthy. Other activities are not as easy to decide about. Today we will study four guidelines that will help you as you look forward to the day when you make more of your own decisions. For now, obey the adults and the others God has placed over you.

See for Yourself

Open your Bible to 1 Corinthians 10:31. Read it carefully and then tell what the guideline is for choosing what we should eat, drink and do. What is it? We are to do all to the glory of God. The guideline could be said this way: *Does this glorify God?* The word "glorify" means to honor, to think highly of. The point is that what we eat, drink and do as Christians causes other people to either think more highly of the Lord or to look down on Him. Our desire should be to lift Him up. What we do is not only important to us but to the Lord, too. It is a good test for a potential activity. Be honest as you answer. It doesn't profit you or anyone else to be deceitful.

Guideline 2 is similar and is stated in Colossians 3:17. What do you read there? Do everything in the name of the Lord Jesus, giving thanks to God. We could put it this way: *Can you do this in the name of Jesus?* Before you go or as you are participating, would it be appropriate to pray for the Lord's blessing on what you are doing? Remember, as a believer the Holy Spirit lives in you and thus goes everywhere you go. Would you feel comfortable taking the Lord Jesus as your guest? If you answer yes, then do ask for God's blessing, go and enjoy yourself. If your answer is no, or I'm not sure, find something else to do. Easy enough to talk about; hard to live!

First Corinthians 6:12 brings out our next guideline. It is a good one. See for yourself: What did Paul say about his activities? Everything is permissible but not everything is profitable or harmless. Some activities which are not bad in themselves dominate the one doing them. Paul said he won't have anything controlling him. The guideline is: *Does it control you or do you control it?* There may come a time when you will choose not to do an acceptable activity because it gets the best of you. This is not easy to understand. Paul wanted so much for everything he did to be of profit to his life. He was really serious about making his life count for God.

Finally, we will read from Hebrews 12:1. This verse

describes life as a race. The Christian is surrounded by a large number of spectators—people who watch his life. We know that sin is wrong and should be laid aside. Sin has no place in the Christian's life; that is evident to all. But this verse also tells the runners to put something else away. What is it? They are to lay aside the weights. Weights are not wrong, but they are heavy and they slow us down in our race. Guideline four is: *Is this wise?* Is this the best way that I can use my time? Does this make me stronger or weaker for God? Will it push me to grow in my love for God? Those are all ways to apply guideline four to a specific question you have about an activity. If the activity isn't profitable and won't help you, you don't have time to do it. If you want your life to count for God, you will have time to do those things that help you grow.

Live It

Don't wait until you are grown to practice these guidelines. Right now you can begin making preliminary decisions. Think it through and then share what you are thinking with an adult. If your parent disagrees with your decision, you are responsible before God to obey your parent. You will not have wasted your thinking—you'll be wiser. When the time comes to begin making choices, you will make wise decisions, not selfish ones.

Ask yourself: (1) Does this glorify God? (2) Can I do it in Jesus' name? (3) Can I control it? (4) Is it wise? Don't be fooled into thinking that only the "big decisions" are important. Your life will be a combination of all the little, everyday things you choose. Make your life count for God! Do the wise, profitable things!

To the Instructor: Make It Visual

Have each guideline written on pieces of cardboard or poster board. Reveal them one at a time as the students find them and identify them. A pocketboard is useful for displaying the key points. They should look like this:

DOES THIS GLORIFY GOD ?

CAN I DO IT IN JESUS' NAME ?

CAN I CONTROL IT ?

IS IT WISE ?

BEGINNING TO PRAY

Scripture Text: *"Evening, and morning, and at noon, will I pray, and cry aloud: and he shall hear my voice" (Ps. 55:17).*

Lesson Aim: The student will be able to address and compose a prayer to the Lord using "dear Father, I am sorry, thank You, in Jesus' name, Amen."

Are You Ready?

"Call Mr. Miller and order the workbooks," requests the manager. "But what do I say?" responds the new employee to the request. "John, you need to write to Grandpa and thank him for your birthday money," instructs John's mother. "I want to, Mom, but what do I say?"

Knowing what to say can be a problem. It's not that you don't want to talk, but you're not sure what is right to say or how to say it. You may not have talked before with the person, so you may not know each other very well. That is a lot like a problem new Christians have.

Many new Christians have this difficulty with prayer. It's not that they don't want to talk to God. More likely they just don't know what to say. They don't know how to get started and how to end. We will look at answers to these questions today.

See for Yourself

We will begin our study in Luke 11:2. Open your Bible there. Please read to yourself the beginning of the disciples model prayer. How did Jesus tell the disciples to begin their prayers? Jesus was not telling them to repeat this prayer as though it was special or could do something for them. Rather, it was a model, a pattern for them to copy in making their own prayers. They were to begin by saying, "Our Father which art in heaven." What is another way that you could say the same thing? You could begin with: "Our Heavenly Father." We begin by addressing the One Who will hear and answer our prayer—God. We can talk to Him because of a special relationship that is part of that opening. Can you see it? We call Him Father. Only those who are sons of God by faith in Christ have the right to call God their Father.

Another part of our prayer is described in 1 John 1:9. This verse is talking about God and what He does with the sin we confess. Read it and share what you find. If we confess, John begins, He is faithful (He will do it every time) and just (He is fair in forgiving) to cleanse (to make us clean) us from all unrighteousness. What is a way to confess? You can say, "I did this. It is wrong. I am sorry." Does God know about our sin? Yes, He knows everything. Then why do we need to tell Him and say we are sorry? First John 1:9 says, "If we confess, He will forgive." God can't take away and forgive what we won't admit we have done. As you are aware of sin in your life, in prayer tell God you are wrong and tell Him you are sorry. Begin with, "Dear Heavenly Father." Include, "I am sorry" whenever you sin. God will readily forgive you.

Another part that should be in every prayer is described in 1 Thessalonians 5:18. What is it? In everything give thanks, it says. You simply say, Thank You, Lord, for. . . . It is proper to say "thank you." God enjoys giving good things to His children. How good it is when we realize that the good things we have come from God (James 1:17). We have so much.

Include a thank you in every prayer. Let's be thankful children of God, not greedy or ungrateful.

Many of us are good at asking God for things. That is not wrong. In John 14:13–15 Jesus tells us what to ask for. We may ask for anything in Jesus' name. Use your hand as a reminder of who to pray for. The thumb is closest to you—pray for yourself and your needs. Your second finger is your pointer. Pray for those who point others to Christ—pastors, missionaries and teachers. Your third finger is the tallest. Pray for the highest in the land, the president, congressmen, those over you. The fourth finger is a ring finger. Pray for your family and your church family's needs. The last finger is the littlest. It can remind you to pray for the low, the little, the poor. *(This illustration was given by Pastor Russell Camp, January 1981.)*

How do you finish a prayer? The answer is in John 14:13. How are we to ask? And whatever you ask in My name (in Jesus' name) that will God the Father do. We have no right to demand anything from God. We come in Jesus' name. It is only because of Him and His holy life, His death and His resurrection that we dare to come to God. We ask and give thanks and say we are sorry because we believe His work covers our sins.

Live It

When you first began writing letters, how was it? Hard, right? Sure it was. You were new at it and you didn't know what to say. It takes practice to be a good writer. It takes practice to feel comfortable praying. You can only pray to God if He is your Father. Could that be why you don't pray? Do you include "I'm sorry" every time you need to say it? He will forgive—don't hesitate! Do you remember to include "thank You"? Every good gift is from God. Do you close, "in Jesus' name"? Will several students volunteer to pray? Begin the right way. Include a "thank You," a "please help" and "I'm sorry" and close with "in Jesus' name." Let us pray.

To the Instructor: Make It Visual

The teacher could role play being the child who is to write the letter. Have another adult call from outside the room as the adult.

Draw a hand and label the fingers to show what to ask for. If time allows, each student could draw his own hand—a reminder to take home. It would reinforce the thought and have more carry-over value to the student's prayer life. In the weeks that come, do allow students to lead in prayer. Practice does make ease in prayer.

A ready-made visual is available from Bible Club Movement, 237 Fairfield Avenue, Upper Darby, PA 19082. It is an illustrated teaching book entitled: *PRAYER, Learning How to Talk to God.* It is not costly and will be of great help.

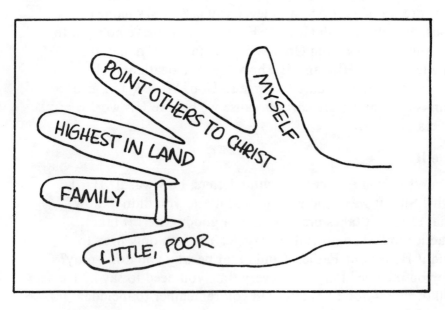

Topical
Specials

GOD'S TIME

Scripture Text: *". . . I have heard thee in a time accepted, and in the day of salvation have I succoured thee: behold, now is the accepted time; behold, now is the day of salvation" (2 Cor. 6:2).*

Lesson Aim: The student will be able to explain that the present is the most important time in God's time for salvation.

Are You Ready?

Tick, tick, tick, tick, . . . the sound of a clock ticking can be very frustrating when you are late or in a hurry. The ticking of the clock is endless. It is a constant reminder that time is passing. There are many games that can be played as a race against the clock. A certain amount of time is given and the players try to run the race or fill the sack or peel the apple. The time limit helps to make the game more exciting and challenging. Every ounce of energy is used in getting whatever must be done, done before the time is gone. Those are enjoyable activities for everyone.

The Bible has many references to time. Psalm 56:3 says, "What time I am afraid, I will trust in thee." A time of fear turned David to rely on God. The prophet Hosea told Israel in Hosea 10:12, ". . . break up your fallow ground: for it is time to seek the LORD. . . ." They had been sinful long enough, Hosea tells them. Turn now to seek the Lord. In Ephesians, Paul tells the saints to buy up every available minute because the times are evil.

See for Yourself

We want to look specifically at God's time. Many people feel that they don't want to be bothered with God right now. They feel that they have many years ahead of them. They do intend to care for their sin problem—but not right now. Do you know anyone like that? Does that describe your attitude? If so, this lesson is for you!

We will check God's "clock" to see what time He says it is. Open your Bible to 2 Corinthians 6:2 and let us read it out loud. Are you ready?

How many time-related words are used in this verse? Name one. There is time, day, now, time, now, day. Six "times" in thirty-four words. Who is speaking? Who is the "he"? You may need to read verse 1 for some help. The voice and words are God's. In fact, He had said this same thing to Israel through the spokesman Isaiah several hundred years before. It is written in Isaiah 49:8. Israel's Redeemer, their Holy One, promised His people who were despised and hated that kings and rulers would worship them. Israel would come on hard times of captivity and slavery but they would also be released. God gave them a promise for that time, "In an acceptable time have I heard thee, and in a day of salvation have I helped thee: and I will preserve thee. . . ." God was aware of their condition. He was allowing them to be slaves for a time as a discipline. Yet, He was still very much in control. In an acceptable, appropriate, right time according to His "clock," what would He do? He promised to hear, to help, to preserve them. Surely that was a sweet promise as they were captives.

How is 2 Corinthians 6:2 different from the verse in Isaiah? Look carefully—and then respond. The first two phrases are nearly identical. The words are rearranged but

86

they mean the same thing. The last part, the "now" section of the verse, is new—Paul's addition to the thought.

Was this the same God speaking to the Corinthians? How do you know? Yes, it was. God never changes. The people were not slaves or captives to a government or foreign ruler. Who were they in slavery to? Yes, they were Satan's, slaves to sin. Paul is using the verse in Isaiah to paint a mental picture. They were not free to serve God while they were slaves to sin.

What has God done according to this verse? He has heard us; He has helped us.

What does "behold" mean? It means attention, please; notice this; this means you. Paul uses it to make the transition from what God said long ago and still means to the topic of right now. Wake up, Paul gently nudges them; don't miss this!

What time-related words are included in Paul's word to them? Now, accepted time, now, day are all used. What time is he talking about? Right now, the *present* is of importance. What is today acceptable for? It is the day of salvation. "Salvation" means to deliver, to bring to safety, to buy back from slavery.

What time is it on God's "clock"? It is the time of salvation.

Live It

How about you? Have you called upon the Lord as Romans 10:13 tells us to do? If you will call today, *now*, God will hear, and He will save you. God's time for you is *now!* Don't wait, don't put off what you know to be right.

But, you say, I have already called upon the Lord. I am saved. He has heard me and helped me to be delivered from sin. First Thessalonians has a word for you. After describing the second coming of the Lord Jesus it says this; listen carefully. (*Instructor read 1 Thessalonians 5:4-6.*) We are not of the night, acting like Satan's people. It says let us not sleep, but watch and be sober minded. We have a responsibility to live differently from others. We are different. We are free to love God, serve Him and watch for Him. Are you loving God? Are you serving Him right now? Are you watching for Him?

To the Instructor: Make It Visual

If your meeting time allows for games, play several which involve the clock. This will accentuate time and also raise excitement and anticipation. Bring a loudly ticking clock to class and allow it to tick for a few moments to make everyone aware of its ticking.

Draw three clock faces and write the question to be answered today on one, the reference on a second and the response on the last. They will look like this:

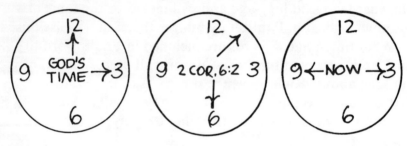

IN MY PLACE

Scripture Text: *"Who his own self bare our sins in his own body on the tree, that we, being dead to sins, should live unto righteousness: by whose stripes ye were healed" (1 Pet. 2:24).*

Lesson Aim: The student will be able to define "substitution" as "to put in place of another." He should be able to explain why Christ's death was one of substitution.

Are You Ready?

We want to talk about substitutes today. Have any of you ever been a substitute? Tell us about it. What made you want to be a sub? (*Allow for a lively discussion. Several will share experiences involving athletic events.*)

Have you ever had a substitute at school? What happened? Why did you have a sub? Probably your regular teacher was sick or had to be away for the day. If your class is like most classes, there was a lot of confusion and noise and very little work done.

What is a substitute? A substitute is put in place of another. We usually think of people as substitutes, but it can mean objects or things, too. What does the Bible say about substitutes? We will look at two verses from the Old Testament and one from the New today in our Bible search. Are you ready?

See for Yourself

In each verse we will be looking for the same information.
We need to discover who is being talked about, who did
wrong and, finally, who received the penalty.

Open your Bible to Leviticus 1:4. It is the third book in
the Old Testament. Read verse 1 to find out Who is talking.
The Lord is speaking to Moses who will relay the message to
the Israelites. What were they bringing? They were bringing
offerings to be killed. The blood of these animals was offered
to God on an altar where it was burned. This is called a
sacrifice. Special instructions about the animal are given in
verses 2 and 3. Who is to lay his hand on the animal's head?
Look at verse 4. The one bringing the animal is to place his
hand on its head. Why do you think he had to do that? He was
showing that this animal was for his sin, for him. By placing
his hand on it, he identified himself with it. Verse 4 says if he
did place his hand on it, something would take place. What is
that? The animal would be accepted for him, in his place, and
make atonement for him. Atonement means payment. The
animal was his substitute.

Who is being talked about? An Israelite. Who was the one
doing wrong—the animal or the man? The man was needing
atonement; thus, he was wrong. Who received the penalty for
his sin? The animal was killed.

Next, open your Bible to Isaiah 53:5. Please read this out
loud with me. Ready? Read. "But he was wounded for our
transgressions. . . ." God is talking here about His servant,
Jesus. Notice how many times "he," "him," "we" and "us"
appear. Let's circle them for a closer look. (*Have the text
written on the board or on an overhead ahead of time; with a
contrasting color, circle all the personal pronouns.*) Five times
a basic thought is stated here. It is substitution. Can you
explain Who the Substitute is and whose place the Substitute is
taking? Jesus is the Substitute and He took our place and the
Israelite's place long ago. Name the five substitutions listed
on the following page.

90

He was wounded	Our transgressions (law breaking)
He was bruised	Our iniquities (sins)
His chastisement (punishment)	Our peace
His stripes	We are healed
LORD laid on Him	Our iniquity

Who is talked about here? Jesus is described. Who did wrong? How easy it is to see that we are the offenders. Who received God's penalty for sin? Jesus did, as our Substitute. How hard it is to believe that He would willingly receive our punishment.

Finally, we will examine 1 Peter 2:24. It is way at the end of the New Testament. Read it quietly to yourself. Again, look for all the words like "his," "our" and "we." What did you find? (*Teacher, have the text written ahead of time to expedite this process. Circle the appropriate words as the students name them to you.*) You should have named his, our, his, we whose and ye. Who does the word "he" refer to? You can tell from verse 21 that it refers to Jesus. Who did wrong? Who was involved in sin? We are the guilty ones. Who took the penalty? Jesus took the penalty. How did He do that according to 1 Peter 2:24? In His own body on the cross He took death for us. What happens to us? We were dead in sin, but we are to live because of the punishment that Jesus took for us. Are you amazed that He would do that for you? Don't be amazed. It is true. You need to be thankful! He is your Substitute.

Live It

Is it fair that the guilty one goes free and an innocent one is punished? No, it isn't fair at all. It is true, though. Have you received Jesus' payment for your sin? Have you told Him how glad you are that He died so that you could go free? Do it right now while we quietly pray.

The story is told of a one-room schoolhouse where the students were quite difficult to manage. The older boys prided themselves on how many teachers they had run out of town.

A new lady instructor arrived one day. She greeted the class and informed them that they were going to have a good school and learn a lot. "Before we begin," she announced, "we will make some class rules together." The students liked that. They eagerly made suggestions for class rules. As they volunteered, the teacher recorded each on the board. "These are fine," she told them. "Now, we will need to determine the penalty for anyone who breaks these rules." More slowly than before the boys determined the penalty for each rule.

Class went quite smoothly for several days with the new class rules and appropriate punishments for each. Then one day Billy, one of the largest and meanest boys, reported that his lunch had been stolen. The punishment for this was fifteen paddles with the belt on the bare back. The boys had chosen the penalty themselves.

"Someone has taken Billy's lunch," announced the teacher. A little boy began to cry. "It was me, Teacher, I took it. I was hungry. I ain't ate nothing for three days. I'm sorry. I won't do it again, I promise. Don't whip me, please."

"I'm sorry, but the rule has been broken and there is a penalty," the teacher softly but firmly reminded him. He rose from his seat and moved to the front of the class. He began to remove his shirt and everyone could see his ribs sticking out.

"Hey, wait a minute, Teacher," Billy yelled out. "The rule says *someone* must get the penalty, but not *who*. I'll take his lickin'. I'm bigger then he is anyway." "OK, if that's what you want, Billy," the teacher responded.

Billy took the lickin' that day for the little boy who had stolen his lunch.

Jesus took your lickin' one day, too, on the cross. He died for you, in your place, as your Substitute. Have you told Him "thank You"?

To the Instructor: Make It Visual

As already explained, have Isaiah 53:5 and 1 Peter 2:24 written out for the class.

Prepare a chart and fill it in as you move along. It should look like this:

VERSE	WHO SINNED?	WHO RECEIVED PENALTY?
LEV. 1:4		
ISAIAH 53:5		
I PETER 2:24		

BOOK OF LIFE

Scripture Text: *"And whosoever was not found written in the book of life was cast into the lake of fire" (Rev. 20:15).*

Lesson Aim: The student will be able to explain what the Book of Life is. He should be able to tell you whether or not his/her name is included there.

Are You Ready?

In this bag are several items. Please tell me what they are and what they are used for. Ready? Here is the first book . . . (*Pull a telephone book out and show for all to see*). Yes, it is a telephone book. It has a list of the phone numbers and addresses of most of the people in our town. In the back are advertisements to tell you all about businesses in town and nearby. Next, here is another item . . . (*Pull a yearbook out for all to see.*) Yes, this is a yearbook. It is a picture record of the people and events of a school year. Finally, what is this? (*Show an autograph book complete with signatures and sayings.*) This is an autograph book, a collection of sayings and the signatures of people who mean a lot to me. Possibly many of you have autograph books of your own.

Today we are going to talk about another book of names. The Bible talks about this book and calls it the Book of Life.

See for Yourself

Exodus 32:30–35 tells about God's book. Follow in your Bible as we read through the passage to get the background of this story. Israel had sinned—it was a serious sin according to Moses' comment. Moses pleaded with God. He confessed the wrong done and asked that they be forgiven. If the Lord would not forgive, what did Moses ask God to do? He requested that his own name be blotted out of God's book. That was a very serious request. Moses felt that if the people were not forgiven, he wanted to be identified with them. He, too, would not be forgiven. What was the reply to Moses? See verse 33. The one who sins is to be held responsible, not someone else. The Lord would punish the people for their sin; Moses' name was *not* to be taken from this book.

Next, we turn to Joshua and a book written for man by God. Open your Bible to Joshua 1:8. We learn from verse 1 that after Moses' death the Lord spoke to Joshua, giving him instructions for being the leader of God's people. What is the name of the book talked about here? The book of the law is named. We know that book was made up of the Bible books of Genesis, Exodus, Leviticus, Numbers and Deuteronomy, already written down and available for Joshua and the people to study.

What were they to do with this book? They were to make it a part of them. They were to meditate on it and to carefully do what they found written there. It is a handbook for prosperous, successful living.

First God's book with Moses' name, next a book of law for man to study and live by. Finally, a book described in Revelation 20:11–15. Turn there and read for yourself what it says about a special book.

The events of Revelation are future events. They are real happenings and will come to pass. John is talking about a scene that he saw in a vision. Describe the scene as it is told here.

There is a throne—it is large and white and a Person is

sitting on it. All the dead, small and great, are there before the throne. Books are opened which contain records of things the dead ones had done. Dead people from everywhere are judged. No one escapes. All are evaluated from the record in the books. There is another book. What is it called? It is the Book of Life. What is recorded in that book? There are names of people there. It is an important book because people are assigned eternal destinations depending on whether their names are there. If your name is written there you inherit Heaven, eternity with the Lord Jesus. If your name is absent, you are assigned to the lake of fire, a terrifying place where there is fire and darkness and torment. The last book is the Book of Life. Is your name in it?

Live It

Jesus told the disciples who followed Him and loved Him, ". . . rejoice not that the spirits [evil spirits or demons] are subject unto you; rather," Jesus said, "rejoice because your names are written in heaven" (Luke 10:20). The idea here is a register of citizens in Heaven.

Paul told the Philippian Christians to help the women who were his co-workers. He said their names were written in this book we studied about in Revelation. It is the Book of Life.

Yes, there is a register of citizens kept in Heaven. The names of all who love the Lord and have received Christ's death as payment for their sins are written there.

Jesus said that some will desire to enter Heaven whose names are not written there. They will even call Jesus "Lord, Lord." He will respond to them, "Depart from me, I never knew you . . ." (Matt. 7:23).

How about you? Is your name written in the register? Do you have a place in God's book? If you answer "yes," rejoice and live like a citizen of Heaven.

If your answer is "no," your name may be written there

96

today! Confess your sin, receive Jesus as your Savior, and He will write your name in the Book of Life.

To the Instructor: Make It Visual

Bring the telephone book, yearbook and autograph book to class in a paper bag. The element of surprise and secrecy will heighten the attention of your pupils. Reveal the books one at a time.

IN HIS LIKENESS

Scripture Text: *"As for me, I will behold thy face in righteousness: I shall be satisfied, when I awake, with thy likeness" (Ps. 17:15).*

Lesson Aim: The student will be able to know that David will be in God's likeness when he sees God face-to-face. He will determine whether he desires a reward now or yet to come.

Are You Ready?

Have you ever carved a pumpkin? It is fun to do, sort of challenging to make a face on it. Have you ever thought that your pumpkin looked like someone you knew? You might have to squint your eyes and imagine a little—but it does look a lot like so-and-so.

Have you ever been told that you have the likeness of someone else? A friend or relative says that you look or act like someone they know. They mean you remind them of another individual known to them. You are either acting or looking much like they do.

Halloween is a time to dress up. We try to make ourselves look like someone or something else. It is a fun time, usually full of laughs. We are taking on another's likeness.

David has a special prayer in the Bible about being in someone's likeness. Today we want to examine Who he says he will be like, how that will happen and how it will make him feel. It is a good study, especially if you will help.

See for Yourself

Open your own Bible to Psalm 17. Psalms is in the middle of the Old Testament. We will read together verses 1 and 6 when you have found the place. What is David saying to the Lord?

He says, "Hear me, listen to my cry, give ear to my prayer," all in verse 1. In verse 6 David adds, "I have called, you will hear, incline your ear to me, hear my speech." All of these comments are a plea for a hearing with God. It is not that David doubts God's desire or ability to hear him. Rather, he is in an *urgent* circumstance and is intent on being heard and receiving help right away. David's repeated call for attention reveals the seriousness of his circumstances, not the inability of God to respond. When we get in a tight spot, all of us can get intense in our praying. David was no exception.

What was David's problem anyway? You will find it in verse 9. David was in danger from the wicked who oppressed him and from the deadly enemies who were all around him. Sounds like a pretty serious state of affairs—both the wicked and his enemies were all around him. David was surrounded. That is a fearful experience! None of us like to be caught there, do we?

David's prayer is a cry for help. Look at verse 13—"Arise, O LORD, disappoint him, cast him down" is his request. As we read on into verse 14, we come to an interesting contrast between the wicked men's fortune and what David was looking for. Each was to receive a reward. One was now; one coming in the future. What are the rewards? Which is the wicked men's and which is David's?

If you read carefully, you should have determined that the wicked have their reward *now*. They have plenty to eat, their children have plenty and more for the little ones. Their reward is in this life—right now. David's reward, recounted in verse

15, is yet future. He will be satisfied, filled full, have plenty. When will this happen to David? When he awakes. The word "awake" means an abruptness in waking from sleep. Sound like a resurrection? It is! The Rapture will be an abrupt waking from sleep.

Why will David be satisfied? When he sees the Lord's Person, he will be satisfied with his likeness. First John 3:2 says it this way, ". . . it doth not yet appear what we shall be: but we know that, when he shall appear, we shall *be like him;* for we shall see him as he is." Not only will David see the Lord, but he will also be in the likeness of the Lord.

In times of trouble, David finds comfort in a yet-to-happen event. When he sees the Lord Whom he loves, he will be like him. David might be in trouble now but he *will be satisfied.*

Live It

How about you? Are you in God's likeness? Do you look like Him? You say, we don't have any pictures, so how can I know? That is true, but is your character, your pattern of behavior like His? You may not be, you cannot be totally in His likeness now because sin is still present and working in you.

Can you be sure, like David, that you will awake in His likeness? If you are a believer, a Christian, you can be. Is your reward right now—a full belly and plenty for your children? Or are you "looking for that blessed hope, and the glorious appearing of the great God and our Saviour Jesus Christ?"

To the Instructor: Make It Visual

This will probably be given during the Halloween season. Many of the illustrations will be part of your decorations. If not, secure a carved pumpkin, a costume of sorts. It will be helpful to have the following key words on large flashcards:

LIKENESS

PSALM 17

URGENT

VS. 1   VS. 6

!! DANGER !!

VS. 9

REWARD NOW

VS. 14

REWARD LATER

VS. 15

IF SHOES COULD TALK

Scripture Text: *"And your feet shod with the preparation of the gospel of peace" (Eph. 6:15).*

Lesson Aim: The student should select from the list those things which best describe his feet. The student should determine and seal with prayer some change regarding the places his feet either should go or should not go.

Are You Ready?

Notice the shoes on my feet. (*Hold up one foot at a time for all to see. Borrow and wear two different shoes. If possible, make them very different in use and season used.*)

Imagine that these shoes can talk. What would they tell you? Why, every day each of us wears something on our feet. And our shoes go everywhere that we go. If only these shoes could talk, they would tell you every place that I have been, all the things that I did in them. They could tell you quite a story about me. They could tell what I spend my time doing.

Shoes leave footprints if you walk in the snow or sand or soft dirt, or even on a clean floor! They leave a mark just like themselves wherever they may go.

(*Tell a story based on the kind of shoes you are wearing. Be alive, creative and energetic. Your students will catch your attitude.*)

You can tell a lot about a person by the kind and

condition of what is on his feet. The Bible has much to say about feet and the lives of those they belong to. Come along and look for the description of your feet.

See for Yourself

We will talk about eight different kinds of feet today. (*If you are pressed for time, you may desire to assign the verses to different girls/boys. Each reads his or her verse to the group, while the others listen and pick out the information needed.*) Each tells us something about the person they belong to. As we learn together what they are, watch for the characteristics that best describe your feet and you.

We begin in Proverbs 1:15, 16. Open your Bible and read together with me. What do the feet do that are described here? They are quick to shed blood and to do *evil*. What kind of a person do they belong to, do you suppose? They are wicked, evil men. What is the instruction given? Don't walk with them.

Psalm 56:13 tells of our next set of feet. Read it aloud, please. What happened to these feet? They were falling and needed to be delivered. Why did David want to be kept from falling? He desired to walk before God. What kind of feet did he want? He requested *delivered feet*. What kind of man would those feet belong to? They would be a godly man's feet.

Our next feet are in Psalm 119:105. What do these feet have? They have a light. Let's call them *enlightened feet*. What does their light come from? "Thy word," the text says. It means the Bible, God's written Word for us. It lights our feet and our path, too. What kind of a person would these feet belong to? One who knows the Bible and uses it to guide his life.

Open your Bible to Proverbs 4:26, 27. Read to yourself what you find written there. What is the first word? "Ponder." What does it mean? It has the idea of watch, take notice, be aware of what way your feet are going. We will call these the *pondering feet*. What should be the result of the pondering of our feet and path? If we do ponder our feet and path, our way will be established or be firm. We will also stay on the right track—not going off to left or right. Finally, we will be kept from evil. There is a threefold benefit to him who ponders his path. How about you? Do you ponder or do you rush ahead, not thinking where your path will take you? What kind of a person will have pondering feet? A careful, thoughtful man who wants to go God's way. Does that describe you?

Isaiah 52:7 is our next stop. This talks about our *beautiful feet!* Interesting—there are not many beautiful feet if you are looking only at physical beauty. Many people have twisted toes, funny nails, bumps and lumps, corns and calluses. What makes feet beautiful according to Isaiah? Those that bring good news, that announce peace and salvation. The feet are only the carriers. The person is really the focal point here. One who publishes good tidings, who tells of God's salvation, has beautiful feet. They are not beautiful to look at but beautiful in what they accomplish. How about your feet? Are they Isaiah's kind of beautiful?

Read Psalm 122:1, 2. Where were these feet going? They were enroute to Jerusalem to the house of the Lord. What do you think would be done at the house of God? They would probably offer sacrifice, worship, sing and praise God. They are *worshiping feet.* They bring their owner to the place of meeting with God. How did the owner feel about going to Jerusalem? He was glad! He wanted to go—and his feet took him.

Our last two examples are in the New Testament books of Matthew and Luke. First, turn to Matthew 18:8. What does this foot do? It offends the owner, keeping him from coming to Christ and receiving eternal life. What is the advice given for those *offending feet?* They are to be cut off. That is strong talk, but the point is, don't let your feet or anything keep you from Jesus. This tells us something of the awful nature of hell fire—it is better to be maimed than to go there. Do your feet offend? Do they keep you from Christ?

Finally, there's the story of a man whose feet experienced

a radical change. Read Luke 8:27 for the "before" and 8:35 for the "after" account of his feet. What were they doing "before"? They were living near the dead ones; they were controlled by Satan's power. How about after Jesus met him and cast out the evil spirits? He was sitting near Jesus, the living God. Before he had been naked, now he was clothed. Before he ran among the graves, now he sat near Jesus and was in his right mind. This man had *learning, quiet feet.*

Live It

We have seen evil feet, delivered feet, enlightened feet, pondering feet, beautiful feet, going to worship feet, offending feet and, finally, learning, quiet feet. Review the list carefully. Now review your life and determine which kind(s) of feet are most like yours.

If your feet are evil, ask God to forgive you and don't walk that way any more. Are your feet delivered? You may ask God, as David did, to keep you from falling. He is anxious to answer that prayer.

Do you memorize the Bible? If you do you'll have enlightened feet. Take time to ponder your path—the Lord will help you to stay on the right one.

Are your feet beautiful? Do you tell others the good news of salvation? You can. Pray for assistance, opportunity and courage to witness.

Do your feet bring you often to the house of God? They should—you can make the choice today.

Do your feet offend, leading you into evil and sin? Ask for God's forgiveness today—don't delay.

Are your feet always running? It is not wrong to run, but your feet need to be learning, quiet feet at times, too.

Take time now for prayer, privately. Talk to the Lord about your feet.

To the Instructor: Make It Visual

Wear unusual shoes to class to spark discussion and help

set the climate. Display each text and the corresponding type of feet on a flashcard shaped like shoes. See sample below:

Either record your findings on the chalkboard as you progress or prepare a flip chart visual. This is especially necessary for the final time when the pupils are reviewing. They need to be able to see them all at a single glance.

Do allow time for prayer and be ready to assist some who need or want to have further help after you dismiss. Be sensitive to your pupils and encourage them to take the steps necessary to fulfill their intentions.

I LOVE MY TEDDY

Scripture Text: *"But God commendeth his love toward us, in that, while we were yet sinners, Christ died for us" (Rom. 5:8).*

Lesson Aim: The student will be able to explain that he is of value to God because God loves him. Given Romans 5:8, the student should be able to tell what God did to show His love for us; namely, He sent Christ to die for us.

Are You Ready?

"Are you any good?" a father asked his six-year-old daughter, Joyce. "No," she responded, "I guess I'm not *much* good." "I wonder," her father asked with a twinkle in his eye and a hug, "why we keep you around here?"

Joyce knew her dad was teasing. He greatly loved her and she him. "Oh, I suppose because mother loves me!" Joyce and her dad both laughed and hugged each other. Joyce was of great value for she was deeply loved. She was valuable not for what she could do but because her mom and dad loved her.

Take a look at this teddy bear. How much would you say he is worth in dollars and cents? Not very much! Why? He's a little worn, has a defuzzed ear and one eye is gone. How much do you think he is worth to his owner? A lot, for sure. He is a companion, a friend; he is loved and that gives him great value.

107

Did you know that we are of great value to God? Not for what we do. We are all sinners, full of shortcomings. Let's look and see what the Bible says about God's love for us.

See for Yourself

We will begin in Romans 3:10. Open your Bible to that place and read with me through verse 18. Notice what this says about our ability to please God with our deeds. What does it say about us?

> None are righteous—or right living (v. 10)
> None understand (v. 11)
> None seek God (v. 11)
> All are gone out of the way (v. 12)
> All are unprofitable (v. 12)
> None do good (v. 12)
> Throat is open grave (v. 13)
> Snake's poison is in mouth (v. 13)
> Full of cursing and bitterness (v. 14)
> Feet shed blood (v. 15)
> Destruction and misery mark their way (v. 16)
> Don't know peace (v. 17)
> Don't fear God (v. 18)

God surely cannot love us for any of these reasons! What a miserable description. Words like "none," "not one," "all" appear repeatedly. We are all included—no escaping. After reading and listing those qualities, I ask you: What value are you to God?

Not much, you say! Oh, but you are wrong. Open your Bible to Romans 5:8. The word "commendeth" here means to show or demonstrate. Read the verse out loud, slowly. What does it say God shows?

God shows His love. To whom does He show love? His love is directed to us, to you and me. When did God show His love for us? It was while we were sinners.

The sinner is the enemy of God—a man, woman or young one set against God and God's ways. This is amazing! God shows love to sinners. He doesn't wait until we love Him and do everything just right. That would never happen. He loves us while we hate Him, while we run from Him, while we curse Him. What special love that is. It is God's love!

God does more than love us with words—Romans 5:8 tells of His love in action. What did He do to show His love? Christ died for us. Christ was the Holy One of God, a holy God-Man Who came and gave His life for ungodly men. This must be love; nothing else could cause Him to do it. God's love was specific. It was directed to *us*! Christ died for the sins of the world, yes, but He also died for you and me specifically. Fill in the verse with your name. Say it out loud right now: "But God commendeth his love toward us, in that, while we were yet sinners, Christ died for _____ ."

Are you of value to God? Yes, yes, yes! Why? Because Christ died for you and God loves you.

Live It

Do you believe that you are of value to God? You are! Do you feel like you are of value to God? You are whether you feel like it or not. Do you act like you are loved by God? Not cocky or uppity but in a loving, kind way you act sure that you belong to God. If you are a believer, act like you are a valuable possession to God. Keep yourself from sin and wrong. Christ paid a high price for you; don't act cheaply.

If you are not yet a believer, do you realize that God loves you just like you are? Without any changes, any reformation, He wants *you*. Admit that you are of no value in yourself and receive His love gift of Christ's death. John 3:16 states very clearly what you need to believe and act on. "For God so loved the world [that means you!], that he gave his only begotten Son, that whosoever [that means you, too] believeth in him should not perish [if you don't believe, you will die], but have everlasting life."

To the Instructor: Make It Visual

Bring a well-worn teddy bear to class for the opening discussion. You may want to display several items with pretend price tags during a presession time. Discuss prices and values with your students.

Encourage the students to use their *own* Bibles and to turn to each passage and follow with the discussion. Do allow time for them to answer. If you rush in with answers, the students will get the idea that you really don't want them to respond. Allow them to take part. Build on their answers. Don't allow them to guess. Send them back to the text for answers, encouraging them to see for themselves.

TAKE A WALK THIS SUMMER

Scripture Text: *"But if we walk in the light, as he is in the light, we have fellowship one with another . . ." (1 John 1:7).*

Lesson Aim: The student should be able to list three of the four ways to walk with God; namely, upright, humbly, worthily, honestly. The student should be able to explain that walking with God is his everyday living.

Are You Ready?

Do you like to hike? Do you enjoy taking a walk with a friend? Where do you go hiking? When do you go? Do you like to go alone or with a friend? (*Allow for discussion and sharing. Students love to tell about things they have done. Each student should share briefly so that many can have a turn.*) Now, let me tell you about a walk I took once. (*Share about a hike or walk you have taken. Tell where you were, who went with you, why it was special.*)

Summer is coming soon. You will be out of school and have more time to do things that you enjoy. Sometimes when we have a lot of free time we don't get anything done. And often students take a spiritual vacation in the summer. They don't take time to go to church or Sunday School. They quit learning. Today we are going to talk about how you can take a walk this summer that will be enjoyable and will benefit your spiritual life. Ready for instructions?

See for Yourself

Walking is a natural activity for healthy people. All of us walk each day. We may not go for long walks but we do walk from place to place. Walking is even good for people who have been sick and are getting well.

When we talk about taking a walk with God, we are using that as a picture. You won't actually take God's hand and go for a stroll. But every day as you do your activities you can do them with God. He can be right with you even though He is not visible or touchable. He is real and wants to be a part of everything you do. To walk with God is to be aware of His presence and to live as He instructs.

To walk with God is to live with Him and with His help. Psalm 116:9 talks about walking. Where does the writer say he will walk? He says he will walk before the Lord, in the land of the living. What does "the land of the living" mean? You could say in the world—in your town. We are to walk or live before the Lord, but we are surrounded by people watching. Listen to 1 John 1:7, "But if we walk in the light, as he is in the light, we have fellowship one with another. . . ." Where are we to walk? We are to be in the light. Who else in that verse is in the light? It says, "he," and it means Jesus Christ.

Is it safer to walk in the day or night? Why? In the day it is easier to see other people, cars, danger and obstacles than at night. Night walking is dangerous without a lamp or flashlight. Light in the Bible is a picture of right and darkness is a picture of sin and evil. Where are we to walk? In the light and in the land of the living.

Who will be your companion if you are in the light? God will be there because ". . . God is light, and in him is no darkness at all" (1 John 1:5).

How do we walk or live with God? There are four special

Bible verses each of which gives us help here. They are
Proverbs 10:9, Micah 6:8, Ephesians 4:1 and 1 Thessalonians
4:12. Look them up and find *one* key word in each about
walking. (*You may need to divide the group to do different
ones for time's sake. If so, share with the total group what
each finds.*)

	Key Word	Meaning
Proverbs 10:9	Upright	Complete, integrity, unbroken
Micah 6:8	Humbly	Not proud, lowly
Ephesians 4:1	Worthy	Value, merit, count for something
I Thessalonians 4:12	Honestly	Becoming, like a Christian

God clearly intends for the Christian's "walk" to be
upright, humble, worthy and honest.

A question that may be in your mind is this: Why should
I walk with God in the light, and be upright, humble, worthy,
and honest? It is a fair question to ask. We need to return to
1 John 1. Follow along with me beginning at verse 5. God is
light and not darkness. We claim to belong to Him; we call
ourselves Christians, followers of Christ. We are lying if we
live in darkness and sin while we claim to follow One Who is
always in the light. The reason we are to walk with Him, in
His way, is because we belong to the Lord Jesus.

OK, you say, it makes sense, but I'll wait till I'm grown,
till fall, till I get older to begin. I want to wait awhile. Do you
recall 1 John 1:6? If you put off walking in the light, you are a
liar. Your life is telling a lie. You are saying, "I belong to
Jesus," but you are living like you belong to the devil. You are
deceiving or fooling yourself.

Live It

First John 1:9 says you need to confess that as wrong. It is a bad attitude. Even worse, if you won't tell God you are sorry and be forgiven, you make God a liar. He says those in the light walk that way. You are saying with your life, I am in the light and I do evil, dark things. Someone's not telling the truth. If you insist on your way, it makes God appear to be telling a lie. That is a serious course of action.

If you are a believer, begin your walk this summer. Live your life uprightly, humbly, worthily and honestly. What are some ways that you can do that? When should you begin? Right now, of course! If you do, you'll have great company—other believers and God Himself!

To the Instructor: Make It Visual

On pieces of construction paper shaped like shoe prints, display the key thoughts of the lesson. Trace your own shoe or sneaker for the pattern, using both right and left feet. You will need four of each. Using masking tape doubled over to be sticky on both sides, display them one at a time as the lesson progresses. Review often; as you add each new one, retrace earlier "steps." They will look like this:

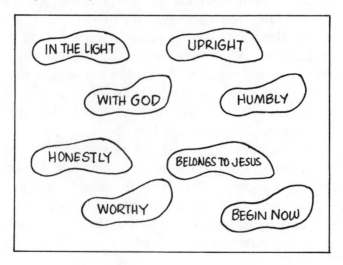

LORD, SEND ME

Scripture Text: *"Then said Jesus to them again, Peace be unto you: as my Father hath sent me, even so send I you" (John 20:21).*

Lesson Aim: The student will be able to tell that *God* sends men. The student who is a Christian will realize that God has a place for him/her to go for Him.

Are You Ready?

Which of you would like to go for me? Do you want to know where? Do you want to know how long it will take? You may like to know what I want you to do. If you asked those questions you are normal and wise. We want to know what is involved and what it will take to do something before we jump in and say "Yes, yes, I'll go."

Do you know this song? "Lord send me, here am I send me, I want to be greatly used of thee. Across the street or across the sea; here am I, oh, Lord, send me." It is the chorus of a hymn used in missionary and youth conferences. The one who sings it or says it is expressing a willing attitude to God to go to the place of His choosing whether it be across the street or across the sea.

Today we are going to talk about several Bible verses and what each has to say to Christians about being sent by the Lord.

See for Yourself

The first part of our study involves five Bible verses. You will not have time to look at each one but do as many as you can. (*The teacher should assign at least one verse to each student so that all verses are covered at once.*) As you find the verses and read them, answer these questions: (1) Who is sending? (2) Who was sent? (3) Where did they go? and (4) Why did they go? What was their purpose? (*Allow time and assistance for all who need it. Provide work sheets, pencils and extra Bibles.*) Here are the verses: Genesis 45:4, 5; Exodus 3:1, 10; Numbers 13:1, 2; Nehemiah 2:5, 6; Isaiah 6:8.

Your completed chart should look like this:

Verse	Who sending?	Who sent?	Where sent?	Why sent?
Genesis 45:4, 5	God	Joseph	Egypt	Preserve his brothers' lives
Exodus 3:1, 10	God	Moses	Pharaoh	Deliver message and His people
Numbers 13:1, 2	God through Moses	12 men	Land of Canaan	Search the land
Nehemiah 2:5, 6	King	Nehemiah	Judah (Home)	Rebuild the city wall
Isaiah 6:8, 9	God	Isaiah	To people of Israel	Tell the people

Now look at the chart and let's make some summaries from what you have found. Who was doing the sending? Again and again you see God sending different ones. God sent Moses or Moses would not have returned to Egypt's court. Sometimes He used men to send other men but the other men were doing as He wanted. Take for example the story in Numbers. A spy mission was to be done. The Lord told Moses, who then did the actual sending. But, while Moses was the

116

man sending them, they were going for God. Moses was the middleman. God sent Joseph; his cruel brothers didn't. God turned an ungodly king's heart to allow Nehemiah to return from captivity, for a time, to Jerusalem. God sent Isaiah to a hard-hearted people.

What sort of people were sent? What can you tell me about the character of each one? (*Allow them to tell what they know and fill in the gaps.*) Joseph loved God and resisted temptation. Joseph stood for his God in a society that hated his God. Moses was chosen by God. He was a miracle baby, protected by God in a special way for a special task.

The twelve spies were choice men, rulers, leaders in their families. They were men who loved God and believed Him. Nehemiah was a man of great importance in a foreign government. He had a deep love for his homeland and his people. He was a tenderhearted man who cried when he heard of the terrible destruction to his country. Isaiah was God's special prophet. He talked to the people for God. He had a long and holy life.

How would you summarize that long description? They were all men who loved God. Their lives were clean, good examples of godly living. God sends men who love Him and who live for Him.

Look at the places they were sent. How many are the same? None; each is different. Each was a place especially prepared for the one sent. God knows us individually. He know our needs, abilities and interests. Remember, He made us the way we are; He will send us to a place just right for us.

Examine why each was sent. Do you see similarities or differences? They are quite different. One went for his family's sake. Moses and Isaiah had messages to deliver but the messages were different. Some were to spy and return with a report. Nehemiah was to direct a building project. Here again we see God's all-knowing plan. He calls the right man for just the right job. He uses wisdom in His assignments and appointments of men to accomplish certain tasks. We have learned that God sends godly men to a variety of places to do a variety of good works for Him.

Live It

Open your Bible now to John 20:21. Jesus is talking to the disciples right after His resurrection. Read what He tells them. Who had sent Him? The Father, forever in Heaven, had sent Jesus. The word "sent" there means to dispatch, to thrust, to send on a temporary errand. That is most interesting. What was His temporary errand? He was to die for man's sin and be resurrected. Where was He sent? Earth was His destination. We have already talked about why He came. Can you recall? Reread the verse. What word or words could you put in place of "even so"? Is it correct to say, "in the same way—just the same"? Yes, Jesus was now the Sender. Who was He going to send? The disciples were now going to be dispatched on a temporary errand.

The reasons why and where they were to go are recorded in Mark 16:15. Read the verse and find the "why" and "where." They were to go to all the world. They were to preach the gospel, the good news about Jesus, to every person. The book of Acts tells us how these men did just what Jesus sent them to do. They went to different places but each did his part in telling the gospel.

If you are a believer, the Lord wants to send you, too. Do you have a clean, holy life? Remember, God only uses clean people. He will send you to a place just right for you. It may be across the street. Later He may send you a longer distance and, still later, to a foreign people. He will send you where you will best be able to work. He will give you a job that no one else can do.

Will you respond with Isaiah, "Here am I, send me"?

To the Instructor: Make It Visual

A large wall chart made from poster board or shelf paper should be prepared to record the individual's Bible-search findings. Each pupil needs his own chart prepared by stencil or mimeographed or by hand if you have a small number of students. A sample is given on page 116 in the lesson.

Appropriate songs for preparation or conclusion include: "Go and Tell the Story," "Lord Send Me," and "Thank You, Lord," chorus with the following words:

"Help Me, Lord, to witness for thee
Help me, Lord, to set others free
Help me, Lord, to pray, give and go
For my Redeemer Who loves me so."

Who Is
Jesus Christ?

CREATOR AND SUSTAINER

Scripture Text: *"For by him were all things created, that are in heaven, and that are in earth, . . . all things were created by him, and for him: And he is before all things, and by him all things consist" (Col. 1:16, 17).*

Lesson Aim: The student will be able to identify Jesus as the Creator of all and as the Sustainer. Using a Bible, the student should be able to list five of the eight areas of His creation from Colossians 1:16.

Are You Ready?

Have you ever seen God with your eyes? If you answered honestly, you said no. The Bible tells us that no man has seen God at any time. Yet men and women of all places and times have been curious about Him. They want to know what He is like, what He does and why He does what He does.

Listen to these words from John 10:30 as Jesus speaks to the Jews. "I and my Father are one." He claims here to be related to God. What is the relationship? He claims to be the Son and God is His Father; He further claims to be the same as God! The Jews didn't like what Jesus said. In hot anger, they took stones to kill Him. Jesus argued that the works which He did were proof of His identity (John 10:38). The Jews still were not convinced and again they tried to grab Him. He escaped from them, however, and from an early death.

We will be studying for the next eight lessons the Person of Jesus. As we learn about Him we are really learning more about God, because Jesus did in the past what He is doing today and what He will do in the future. Jesus reveals or shows us what God is like, what God does.

Jesus Christ was a genuine flesh and blood man. The four Gospel accounts talk of Him almost exclusively. By studying clues in the New Testament letters to the churches, we can determine His work in the past and future. Today we will discover His work in the beginning of time.

See for Yourself

Open your Bible to Colossians 1:16. First, check the final phrase of verse 13. Whose kingdom is named here? The kingdom of His (or God's) dear Son. We know that Person to be Jesus. You will see that what follows in verses 14–19 all describe this dear Son. What does verse 15 tell us about this Son? He is the image of the invisible God. We have already agreed that God has never been seen with human eyes. He is invisible but His Son is visible. Jesus is the Image, the Likeness, the Representation, the Profile of God.

What does verse 16 say that Jesus did? He created all things. How many things is He the Creator of? *All* things. How do you know that? Because Colossians 1:16 says, "For by him were all things created. . . ." A list follows of the realms created. Can you name eight from verse 16? They are: things in Heaven, things in earth, visible things, invisible things, thrones, dominions, principalities, powers.

Can you name something Jesus created in Heaven? The angels are created beings. So are the planets, the galaxies and the stars. Can you name something Jesus created in the earth? The animals, trees, plants, birds, air, sea creatures, sky and people are all examples of Jesus Christ's creative work. He made the visible things and the invisible, unseen things, too.

What does "create" mean to you? An individual creates when he brings something into existence from nothing. To originate, to design, to bring into being is how Webster defines creating. *Jesus Christ is the Creator.* He was present before Adam and Eve, before the garden, before the dry land, and the sun and moon and stars. He is the Maker of them all.

Check the beginning of verse 17. What does this say about Jesus' beginnings? It says He is before all things. He was real and active in the creation. He was there *before* the world as we know it. Before things in Heaven and earth were made, He was there.

Listen as I read to you John 1:1–3. Every time you hear the words "word" or "him," substitute the name of Jesus. Ready? It should sound like this. "In the beginning was Jesus, and Jesus was with God and Jesus was God. The same Jesus was in the beginning with God. All things were made by Jesus and without Jesus was not anything made that was made."

Did Jesus have help in creation? No, it says that apart from Him nothing was made. He is the Creator. He created everything by Himself.

Focus your attention on the second half of Colossians 1:17. A second name for Christ is described here. What does the verse say? ". . . By him all things consist." The word "consist" means hold together. *Jesus is the Sustainer!* He holds His creation together. He causes it to function, to run consistently and in an orderly fashion. Hebrews 1:3 puts it this way: ". . . upholding all things by the word of his power. . . ." He carries all the creation along by His powerful word. Without His work as Sustainer, the world would fall apart.

Scientists talk of an "atomic glue"—an unknown source of power that holds atoms together in their structure. They do appear to be mysteriously "held together." They are indeed held together by Jesus Christ, the Sustainer. Not only did He cause the worlds to be, but they continue on in His power as well.

Jesus is the Creator of all things everywhere. He is the

Sustainer, the continuing Source of power and "holding together" of all He has made.

Live It

So what, you say, does all of that mean to me? As you look at things around you, do you see only the object—trees, birds, animals, people, beautiful scenery, gorgeous sky, dramatic sunsets—or do you see Jesus' handiwork? Do you see all of these as the work of Jesus Christ? Do you accept Him as the Creator, the great Designer of all you enjoy? Or are you satisfied to just see trees, birds, animals, people, scenery and sunsets? He wants you to know Him, not only His creation.

Are you frightened that the world may fly apart? You need not be, because Jesus is sustaining all He has made. There may be an energy crisis and a shortage of water and other necessary items, but Christ holds all that we know together by the power of His Word. We need not fear because we can place our confidence in Him, the great Sustainer. Are you fearful or are you trusting? He is the Sustainer—share your need with Christ today.

To the Instructor: Make It Visual

A set of prepared visuals for this lesson is distributed by Moody Press, entitled, *Basic Bible Doctrine #4, The Lord Jesus Christ*. Transparency #1 will serve as an excellent visual review and/or introduction to the lesson.

On large 6″ strips prepare the words Creator and Sustainer. Display them after each point is established.

Look through magazines and clip pictures suitable for showing God's creation—people, animals, trees, plants. Check your church's picture file or Sunday School resource for pictures of angels and sketches of Heaven. Write the definition of *Creator* and *Sustainer* on the board for all to see and to review.

GOD IN THE FLESH

Scripture Text: *"And the Word was made flesh, and dwelt among us . . ." (John 1:14).*

Lesson Aim: The student will be able to define "incarnate" as "in the flesh." The student will be able to give at least two reasons why Jesus came in the flesh.

Are You Ready?

Let's see how well you listened and what you understood from our last lesson. Please raise your hand to respond to every question you think you can accurately answer.

- Has anyone ever seen God face-to-face?
  - —No, we cannot. He is too holy and pure; we are sinful.
- How do we know what God is like, then?
  - —The Bible tells us about Him.
  - —Jesus shows us what God is like.
- What does Colossians 1:16 tell you Jesus did? (*Read aloud to class.*)
  - —He created *all* things. He is the Creator.
- Listen to Colossians 1:17. (*Read for all.*) What does "consist" mean?
  - —He holds together His creation.
- What two names did we give to Jesus from Colossians 1:17, 18?

—He is the Creator.

—He is the Sustainer.

We have learned that Jesus was present at creation, at the beginning of time. He was there with God, and He had an active, important part in the beginning of our universe. If that was all we knew of Jesus we would be very limited in our understanding of Him. Can you think of some reasons why we would be limited? (*This is a thought-provoking question. Allow time to think; encourage careful response, not just a repeating of answers they might have heard.*)

If you were shown something that I had made but you never met me face-to-face, you might know something about me. But there are some qualities about me that my work can't show. Which would give you a better understanding of me—seeing my handiwork or living with me for a day? Why? Obviously if you are with me, you could ask a lot of questions, watch what I do, what I don't do, observe how I react, and so on. It is much easier if you are with me. It takes away some of the guessing. Also, it helps me to become more real to you.

God wants you to know Him, too. Today we are going to learn how He provided a way for us to know Him a long time ago. Are you ready to learn about it?

See for Yourself

Open your own Bible to John 1. Last week we read verses 1–3. Let's review and read them aloud together. Now begin again at verse 11 and read through verse 14. Remember, this is talking about the Lord Jesus. Every time you see the words "he" or "his" they refer to Jesus.

We want to look closely at verse 14. Please read the first half of the verse slowly so I may write it on the board.

"And the Word was made flesh, and dwelt among us, (and we beheld his glory, the glory as of the only begotten of the Father) . . ." Who does "the Word" refer to? Yes, it is the Lord Jesus. What do you learn happened to Him? He was made flesh. There is a special word for making someone flesh. It is "incarnate." It is spelled like this. (*Write it on the board for all to see.*) Please say it with me three times. Do you see any smaller words in it that you recognize? Yes, the word "in" is there. Also part of "carnival" or "carnivore." What is a carnivorous animal? A carnivorous animal eats meat, or we could say it eats flesh. Do you know any carnivorous animals? Lions, tigers, dogs, wolves, cats and seals are all examples. To be incarnate means to be in the flesh. It has the idea of being given a body.

Who in John 1:14 was incarnate? The verse says the Word was made flesh. Jesus, Who helped create all the world, was given a body. He was made to be a man. The word "made" in the verse means "to begin to be." Jesus was not always a man; He was not always on earth; He was not always in the flesh. At the time of Mary and Joseph's engagement God worked a miracle. There are not a lot of details given about how this happened; however, the verse is very clear that it *did* happen. It is true. Jesus was made a man.

How can God become a man? How can He take on flesh? I don't know; it is not explained. We wouldn't be able to understand it, anyway. We must believe that it is true. There are a number of ways that we can tell that Jesus was God in the flesh. We may not know how it was done, but we can be sure that it *was* done.

Name some things that Jesus did on earth that only God can do. He did many miracles; He knew things before He was told; He had unlimited power; He said He was God's Son. Name some proofs that He was a man. He was tired; He was hungry; He cried; He was tempted; He died; He ate food; He loved people; He talked and walked with the disciples and others.

John 1:14 tells us that the incarnate Jesus dwelt among us. What does "dwelt" mean? It means to live or make your home there. Jesus left Heaven to come and live on earth. The word "dwell" also means a tent or tabernacle. Have you ever lived in a tent? Would you want to live your whole life there? Why not? It's fun for a short time, but not as a permanent place. It could blow away or fall over. In really cold or rainy weather it wouldn't be warm or dry enough. It is meant to be a temporary living place. You use it for overnight or for a vacation, but not to live in for a long time. Explain how Jesus' body was a tent or temporary living place. (*Do be patient, teacher, while your students formulate thoughts and words! It is necessary for them to think this through on their own. Your explanation should be a summary of the right points they make. Don't jump in too soon, lest they learn that you don't expect them to respond. They need to!*)

Jesus was only intended to live a short time here. His real purpose was to die for us. He was in the flesh. He had a man's body. He intended to live with us—but only for a short time.

What does John say they noticed about Jesus? They saw His glory. What kind of glory was it? It was the kind of glory that belongs only to the begotten of the Father. "Begotten" means born one. Jesus was the only Son of God. The glory they saw was God's glory in His Son—Jesus.

What does "incarnate" mean? Who was incarnate in John 1:14? Was He a man or was He God? He was both!!

Live It

There are four reasons why Jesus was incarnated that we want to talk about. There is a verse for each reason. Please find them in your Bible. We will read each verse and I will tell you the reason. The verses are John 1:18, Hebrews 10:12, 1 John 3:8b and Hebrews 4:15. (*If you are pressed for time, copy the texts on overhead or poster board for all to see.*) Why did Jesus become incarnate?

John 1:18 says the only Son of God hath declared Him. No one has seen God but His Son shows us Who He is. *Reason #1: Jesus became incarnate to show us God.*

Hebrews 10:12 talks about Jesus. He offered a sacrifice for sins. What was Jesus' sacrifice? He gave His blood and His body. If He was not incarnate, He could not die for sin. God cannot die; man can. As the incarnate God-Man, He died for

130

us. Are you thankful He was incarnate? If He hadn't been, you would not have a sacrifice for sin. *Reason #2: Jesus became incarnate to pay for sin!*

Begin in the middle of 1 John 3:8 with, ". . . For this purpose . . ." "Manifested" means to appear. Jesus appeared in a body to destroy the works of the devil. *Reason #3: Jesus became incarnate to destroy Satan's work.*

Finally, Hebrews 4:15 says our High Priest, Jesus, was touched by all the realities of life. All of the hard things, all of the disappointments, all the tests, all the hurts of life touched Him. He is our Counselor. He has known all we experience, yet He was victorious. We can go to Him for help. *Reason #4: Jesus became incarnate to be our Counselor.*

Can you recall all four reasons for the Incarnation?
- To show us God • To pay for sin
- To destroy Satan's works • To be our Counselor

To the Instructor: Make It Visual

Again the Moody overhead series has graphic visuals for this lesson. Transparencies #2 and #3 of *Basic Bible Doctrine #4* are specifically designed for the content presented here. Use a blank sheet to reveal one item at a time, thus building anticipation and sustaining the students' interest.

As the lesson itself mentions, write John 1:14 on the chalkboard for all to see. As you explain key words, circle them and jot down simple definitions. Refer to them often.

Prepare a flashcard with the word "incarnate" on it.

INCARNATE

Use your hand to first cover and then reveal the smaller words within it. Prepare four cards with the reasons why the incarnation is necessary. You will find them given in the LIVE IT section of this lesson.

HIS DEATH FOR US

Scripture Text: *"For Christ also hath once suffered for sins, the just for the unjust, that he might bring us to God . . ." (1 Pet. 3:18).*

Lesson Aim: The student will be able to define three of the four terms describing the death of Christ: ransom, reconciliation, propitiation and substitution. The student will be able to explain why each of these terms proves God's love.

Are You Ready?

We have talked about Jesus Christ as the Creator, the Sustainer and the incarnate Christ. What do those names mean? (*Allow several to answer and bring out the key points studied thus far.*)

There are many special things about the birth and life of Jesus Christ. How many can you list? His birth was unique— He was born without a human father. He was born in a town far from the place where Mary and Joseph lived. He had several unique visitors, including shepherds and learned men from a distant country. His birth attracted a king's attention in spite of His poverty and lowly beginning. Jesus did many miracles. He taught with authority and amazed learned and religious leaders. He attracted huge crowds and many curious followers. He made claims that He was related to God, that He was God. Although these are just a few of the facts about Jesus, they remind us that His birth and life were unique.

Today we will learn about the death of Jesus. Most people don't like to talk about death or dying, and often they refuse to admit that their own death may be near. They would rather focus on living and all that life means and brings to them. Yet the most significant event for Jesus was His death. We will learn four words relating to His death and what those words can mean in our lives.

See for Yourself

How many chapters in each Gospel relate information about the death of Christ? Take time to look at Matthew, Mark, Luke and John, counting the ones that talk of His trial and crucifixion. What do you find? Matthew has two very lengthy chapters (26 and 27), Mark has two long chapters (14 and 15), Luke has two chapters (22 and 23) and John also has two (18 and 19)—eight full chapters in all. Each is written from a different man's viewpoint, yet all focus on the same event. Clearly Jesus' death is the high point, the climax of each of the four Gospel accounts.

Jesus did die. His death is a well-established fact of history. But there is much more at stake here than facts and history. His death has a relationship to your life and your future. Even though He lived and died two thousand years ago, what He did is important for you to think about.

We want to talk today about these words and their meanings: *ransom, reconciliation, propitiation* and *substitution.* They are taught in the Bible. We will define each one, read about it from the Bible and give an illustration of what it means.

Open your Bible to Mark 10:45 and read it aloud with me. "For even the Son of man came. . . ." Who is the Son of Man being talked about here? Yes, it means the Lord Jesus. What did He not come to do? He did not come for people to serve Him. What did He come to do? He came to serve, help, assist others and to give His life as a *ransom*. "Ransom" means to buy back. Some kind of a payment is involved and a person is released from a captor. We hear often in our time about people being held prisoners or hostages. The ones holding them agree to release them in exchange for a certain amount of money or other ransom payment. The ransom is what it costs to set the people free. Ransom is easier to understand when real people and actual money are involved.

Who made us? God did. Who has captured our hearts and lives? Whose prisoners are we? If you said Satan, you are right. Jesus Christ's death was a ransom payment for our release from Satan's power and control. To ransom is to release at the payment of a price. What did it cost Christ to ransom us? His life and His blood are the ransom price.

Our second word is *reconciliation*. It means to bring together two enemies. Open your Bible and read to yourself 2 Corinthians 5:18, 19. Do you see our word "reconciliation" here? Yes, it appears four times. Who are the two people who are reconciled in the opening part of verse 18? *God* reconciled *us* to Himself. The word "us" means the Corinthian Christians and it includes Christians today, too. Jesus Christ is the One responsible for bringing together sinful man and a holy God. How did He do that? His death brought sinful man and God together by paying the penalty for sin. Sin had caused the separation. Sin causes man to be God's enemy, and by ourselves we can do nothing to restore the relationship (Isa. 64:6). Our best efforts fall far short. Only Christ can reconcile us to God; He did that by His death.

Picture reconciliation in this way: Two fists are at a great distance from each other. Now imagine that a third person brings the hands close together and joins them in friendship. This is what reconciliation means.

Our third word is probably new to you. It is *propitiation*. Say it aloud. *Pro-pi-shi-a-tion.* You will find it explained in 1 John 2:1, 2. It means to satisfy someone's anger. Read the verses in 1 John. Who is the propitiation for us? Jesus Christ is our propitiation. What does He propitiate for us? He propitiates our sins and the sins of the whole world.

Romans 1:18 says that the wrath or anger of God is against all ungodliness and unrighteousness. Simply, it says that God hates our sin. He is angry with our disobedience, our rebellion and our sin. He is angered when we break His laws. The punishment for breaking God's law is the sinner's death (Rom. 6:23a). Jesus died to satisfy God's anger over your sins, my sins, and the sins of the whole world. His death satisfied God's law, so God is no longer angry over the sins of anyone who receives Christ's work.

Here is an example. A brother and sister are home alone while mom has gone shopping. The sister trips while playing with her baton and knocks over the lamp. It breaks into many little pieces. She knows her mom will be angry because they have a family rule that batons are to be for outside use only. She has no money, so she can't buy a new lamp. The brother, meanwhile, offers to pay for a new lamp. He didn't break the lamp but he is the propitiation for his sister. His gift will hopefully satisfy their mom's anger.

Finally, Christ's death was a *substitution*. You know what a substitute is. Tell me. A substitute is one who takes the place of another, a stand-in. Read 1 Peter 3:18. The word "substitute" is not used here, but the idea is clearly explained. Who is just? Christ is. Who is unjust? We are. Who should rightly suffer for sins, the just or the unjust? By all rights the unjust should. Who did suffer and die? Christ did. Who was our Substitute? Christ was the Substitute for every one of us.

Live It

Well, there you have it: ransom, reconciliation, propitiation and substitution. Can you tell me what they mean? (*Review definitions carefully.*) Who are sinners ransomed from? They are bought from Satan's control. Who are sinners reconciled toward? They are reconciled or brought back to God. What does Christ propitiate for us? He satisfies God's anger over our sin. Whose Substitute was Jesus? He died in the place of sinful man.

How do these prove God's love? Only love would cause Christ to ransom us. If He didn't love us, He would allow us to continue in sin. Love for the captured one is what makes a ransom work. Do you want to be set free?

Reconciling enemies is painful at best. Only someone who deeply loves both God and man would be willing to die so they could be brought together. Jesus loves you. He died to reconcile you to God. Are you resisting or allowing His work to be done in your life?

In propitiation Christ pays a debt He does not owe for Himself. He pays to satisfy the penalty for your sin. Have you thanked Him? Have you received Him? What love He shows by paying for your offense!

As your Substitute, He died and you go free. Human love isn't strong enough for that kind of sacrifice. Only God's love would cause Christ to die for you—in your place.

To the Instructor: Make It Visual

Moody's *Basic Bible Doctrine #4,* overhead transparencies #4 and #5, are useful for this lesson. Emphys are prepared for #5 to add one at a time for added impact. The emphys further explain the key words studied. Practice with the emphys before you attempt to teach with them.

If you do not have access to the overhead series, gather several pictures from your church's teaching pictures to help remind the students of unique facts about Christ. The pictures could include: nativity, Mary and Joseph traveling, shepherds, wise men, Herod's consultation with wise men, miracles of Jesus.

Prepare the key words on 8½" x 11" sheets and display them prominently in your teaching area. Refer to each repeatedly.

You may try to role-play substitution with another adult

or a student who you may cue in ahead of class. Use your imagination to construct a situation where a penalty is given for an offense. Have the innocent individual offer to take the penalty for the offender.

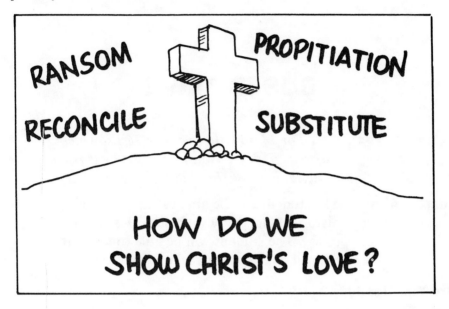

JESUS IS ALIVE

Scripture Text: *". . . For I know that ye seek Jesus, which was crucified. He is not here: for he is risen, as he said . . ." (Matt. 28:5, 6).*

Lesson Aim: The student will be able to explain from historical facts why we believe Jesus is alive today. The student will be able to tell that the resurrection was real and true.

Are You Ready?

(List these words for all the students to see—Creator, Sustainer, incarnate, ransom, reconcile, propitiation, substitute.)

Check these definitions on the board. Give me the right answer from the definitions:

- To buy back from Satan (*ransom*)
- To make everything (*Creator*)
- To be in a human body (*incarnate*)
- To stand-in for someone (*substitute*)
- To hold everything in the universe together (*Sustainer*)
- To bring enemies together (*reconcile*)
- To satisfy someone's anger (*propitiate*)
- To bring into being things visible and invisible, in Heaven and in earth (*Creator*)

All men and women are born. Given enough time and either disease or accident, all will die. The newspapers carry both birth announcement columns and obituaries. Have you ever seen a resurrection column? "Resurrection" means to rise from the dead, to come back to life. When people die we are sad and often cry, realizing that our loved one will not be coming back. Death is final. People don't die and then change their minds.

When Jesus died His friends, close followers, were sad. They loved Him very much. They had given up everything to follow Him and now He was dead, gone; no longer helping or healing. Three days had passed since His awful death on the Roman cross on the hill outside the city. Three ladies had gone to His grave. They were sad, weeping, tired from the hurt they felt at losing Him. Let's read the written record and join them on the way to the graveyard. . . .

See for Yourself

Begin reading with me in Matthew 28:1 and read on through verse 8. Here we read of a most unusual event, with many details given to help prove its factuality. We know exactly which day it was; we know the time of day; we know the names of those who were eyewitnesses. It was the first day of the week, Sunday. It was early morning at sunrise. Mary Magdalene and Mary the mother of James and Joses were on their way to the sepulchre. What is a sepulchre? It is a vault for a grave, an open cave where someone is placed after death.

Describe the place of Jesus' burial. The disciples placed Him in a rock cave in a garden. A heavy stone was rolled to cover the entrance and the Roman soldiers sealed it for security reasons.

What happened at the grave site of Jesus according to verse 2? An earthquake occurred, and an angel came and moved the stone that closed up the cave. Where was the angel when the women arrived? He was sitting on the stone.

Did the angel know why the women were there? See verse 5. Yes, he told them not to be afraid and he knew they wanted to see Jesus Who had died. How did the women know that

139

Jesus was gone from the grave? See verses 6, 9, 10, 17 and 18. Six proofs are given in Matthew 28 to show that He was alive: The angel said it, they were allowed to see for themselves, Jesus met them, Jesus talked to them, they saw Him again, Jesus spoke to them.

What did the angel tell the women to do in verse 7? They were to go quickly and tell the disciples that He was alive. Jesus was to meet them in Galilee.

Did they believe what the angel said? How do you know? Look at verse 8 for help. They did believe Him. They left in a hurry in fear of the angel, but also in great joy. They had come with heavy, saddened hearts; they left in joy! They ran to bring word to the disciples. Only news about Jesus could have caused that change of destination and attitude of heart.

We want to review, now, using these facts from the Matthew account to help show that this was a true event.

First, an empty tomb or grave would prove Jesus' resurrection if:

(1) the ladies had not found the wrong grave;
(2) someone had not stolen the body, maybe disciples;
(3) robbers had not taken His body for a prank.

How would you answer each of these objections? Use your best thinking skills. . . . (*Suggested answers:* (1) The presence of so many guards made the tomb easy to find. (2) Government guards were posted for that very possibility. Besides, the disciples had scattered in fear and hurt. Only the ladies ventured to the tomb. (3) Robbers would have shown the body later to disprove the claims to resurrection. The pieces of grave clothes were neatly placed, indicating a careful, deliberate action, not a theft.)

Second, the many times people saw Jesus alive is proof of His resurrection. See verse 9 of Matthew 28. Jesus met them on their way to find the Twelve. The entire group saw Him in verse 17. Some of them were convinced, some doubted. Jesus convinced them with His words. On the road to Emmaus Jesus showed Himself to two men; He even ate while they watched.

A third evidence of Jesus' resurrection is the impact made by the telling of it. All through Acts, first Peter and later Paul talked about the Lord's resurrection. Some reacted in anger because blame was placed on them, but none challenged the fact. Three thousand believed Peter in one city on one day. Later five thousand and other large numbers of people believed. Those people lived close enough to the event to have occasion to be skeptical. No one had ever risen from the dead. This was an *unusual, unique, one-time event,* yet they were convinced. Many had complete changes of heart and life.

The empty tomb, the appearances, the changed lives all point to this fact: HE IS ALIVE!

Live It

What does all of this mean to you and me? At least three things can be learned from this event established by fact, eyewitnesses and the historical record of Jesus' resurrection. They are the following:

(1) Jesus must be God. He promised to go before the Twelve to Galilee after his death. No man in his right mind makes appointments on earth after the day of His death. Jesus claimed to be God—He kept His word and His appointment (*compare Matt. 26:31, 32 and Matt. 28:16*). Only God has power to raise the dead.

(2) A promised resurrection for ALL is coming! Listen to 1 Corinthians 15:20–24. The same Jesus Who came from the dead will raise all men to be judged by God. We know He has power to do it. He promised it and will do it.

(3) To the Christian, all this means his sins are forgiven, taken away, gone forever. If Jesus had died and that was the end of Him, He would be no different than all other religious men. He claimed to die for sins and He arose to finish the task, declaring victory over death and sin (1 Cor. 15:17, 55)!

141

To the Instructor: Make It Visual

Transparency #6 of Moody's *Basic Bible Doctrine #4* is especially suited to illustrate this lesson's content. Place the stone emphy over the opening until you come to verse 6, then roll it away to reveal the angel's announcement.

At the lesson's beginning, display on the board the matching words for the review. If you do not have the transparency series, make your own wall display out of construction paper and a lettering guide or stencil. A sample is shown below:

HE IS ASCENDING

Scripture Text: *"But ye shall receive power, after that the Holy Ghost is come upon you: and ye shall be witnesses unto me. . . . while they beheld, he was taken up; and a cloud received him out of their sight" (Acts 1:8, 9).*

Lesson Aim: The student will be able to define "ascension" as the return of Jesus to Heaven. The student will be able to name Christ's command and promise as Acts 1:8 records it.

Are You Ready?

We have had four lessons about the Lord Jesus. First, we learned what He did before anything was, before time began. What was that? He was the Creator. That same week we discussed His part in keeping all of creation together. What is His part? He is the Sustainer. The next week we learned a difficult word that means "in the flesh" or in a human body. What was the word? "Incarnate" describes Jesus as the God-Man in human form. We next studied the cross and how it showed Christ's love for us. Can you tell me the definitions of ransom, reconciliation, propitiation and substitution? (*Allow time for responses.*) Fine, you have listened and remembered well. What do we call Jesus' coming back to life? Yes, it was a resurrection. Will you and I ever be resurrected? If we die before Jesus comes, He will bring us back to our bodies.

Now, how do you think the disciples felt when they saw Jesus alive again? (*Allow a number of students to respond before moving on. This role-taking will help the student identify emotionally with the Twelve.*) Jesus their Friend, their Lord and Master, had died and was alive again! I think I would have felt _____ (fill in your own thoughts here).

If someone you loved very much left you and then returned, would you be afraid he might leave again? I would. It seems to me that the disciples would have hung on every word and spent every available moment with Jesus. Today we will learn about the second time He left them—we will see it from their eyewitness account. Open your Bible to Acts 1.

See for Yourself

Today we will learn about the ascension of the Lord Jesus. Would you say it with me, please (a-sen-shun). What does "ascend" mean? It has the idea of going up, moving upward. We might talk today about ascending a set of stairs, ascending a hill or ascending a mountain. Acts 1 records Jesus' going up to Heaven. We call it His ascension.

Read out loud with me the first eight verses to get the scene. The word "treatise" in verse 1 means book. Dr. Luke had written first the Gospel of Luke and now Acts to a man named Theophilus. The first book, we are told in verse 1, contained what Jesus did and said. This second book begins where the first left off—namely, the ascension of Jesus. Do you see the definition of ascension in verse 2? What is it? He was taken up.

We have eight questions to answer from these verses. Look carefully for the answers and please tell where you find them.

(1) Who saw Jesus (vv. 2, 3)? _____ We are told that the apostles whom He chose saw Him. Jesus not only met with them, but showed through many infallible proofs that His resurrection was real and genuine.

(2) How long did they see Him (v. 3)? _____ For

144

forty days He was with them. For a few minutes or hours an imposter could have fooled them. Not so with Jesus. He was with them for a month and ten days, proving His Person and claim to genuine life.

(3) What was Jesus' command (v. 4)? _____ They were to wait for the promise of the Father. The word "wait" means to stay or remain in one place. Jesus knew their needs better than they. In a time of trouble they might have scattered and run. He instructed them to stay together in Jerusalem, anticipating a promise from the Father.

(4) What were they *not* to know (v. 7)? _____ They were not to know the times or the dates of the coming kingdom. Jesus had promised to set up a ruling monarchy with Himself as King. They had felt that with His death all hopes for that were gone. Now, with their Lord alive, surely He would set up the kingdom. The disciples talked together about the kingdom but Jesus talked of something else.

(5) What would they have (v. 8)? _____ They were to receive *power* to witness. The Person of the Holy Spirit would come upon them as they waited in Jerusalem. He would bring power or authority and put areas under their control. They were to be witnesses, or records, of the truth about Christ's death and resurrection to others in the city where they were, in the surrounding region, in nearby nations and eventually to all the world. Surely they would need power to accomplish all that.

(6) What happened while they watched (v. 9)? _____ Jesus was taken up. He began to ascend. It was as though someone were invisibly lifting Him away from them. A cloud took Jesus almost as if it were a supernatural elevator. It transported Him from their sight, up and away from them. They must have looked very intently, determined to see where He went, all the while hoping that He would come back while they watched. Again their beloved Lord was gone!

(7) Who stood by the disciples (v. 10)? _____ Two men dressed in white, no doubt angels sent to comfort, were

standing alongside them. They didn't yell from Heaven. They stood shoulder to shoulder with them to encourage them.

(8) What was their message (v. 11)? _____ This same Jesus will come back from Heaven. Their message was comforting. This same Jesus, this resurrected, alive, real Lord will come. He is in Heaven now—He will come from Heaven in the future. They must have been comforted. We read later in Acts 1 that they followed the command Jesus had given to wait in Jerusalem.

Live It

These men loved Jesus; they mourned His death. They had been deeply hurt at His torture and cruel death by crucifixion. They had scattered, hiding lest *their* lives be taken, too. They had given all to follow Jesus. His death, even though necessary, had shattered them.

Then He was alive! Again they talked and fellowshiped together! Again He was with them. They ate, they talked, they questioned Jesus. In a final meeting He had given them a command—something to do—and a promise, to keep them going. What was the command? "Be My witnesses," He told them. "Tell others everywhere what you have seen and know to be true." What was the promise? "I will come again."

The first time Jesus left they scattered; now they stayed together and waited. They would need power and Jesus would send it. What a changed group of men. Once they ran and hid; now they waited and prayed!

What about you? Are you a follower of Jesus? If you say yes, then you too have a command and a promise. Be His witness—tell what you know to be true about Him. Hang on to His promise to return for you! He is coming just as He went.

If you don't know Christ, His command isn't for you. You have nothing to tell until by faith you receive Him. Neither is the promise for you. He is coming for His own—He may come today. Won't you receive Him?

To the Instructor: Make It Visual

Transparencies #7 and #8 from *Basic Bible Doctrine #4* and the emphy "Jesus" are for this lesson's visual impact. Use them as the instructions indicate for added visualization. If you cannot obtain the transparencies, use a teaching picture of the ascension, pointing out salient features.

Prepare the list of eight questions in brief on a chalkboard or overhead sheet (*see pages 144 through 146*). You may desire to use a pocketboard and place the questions one at a time. This will help to build suspense and keep the group together.

Your visual will look like this:

```
+------------------------------------------------------------+
|                    HE IS ASCENDING                         |
|                                                            |
|   Who saw Jesus _____   |
|                                                            |
|   How long _____   |
|                                                            |
|   Command _____   |
|                                                            |
|   Don't know _____   |
|                                                            |
|   Will have _____   |
|                                                            |
|   While watching _____   |
|                                                            |
|   Who stood by _____   |
|                                                            |
|   Message _____   |
|                                                            |
+------------------------------------------------------------+
```

RELATED TO CHRIST
(Part I)

Scripture Text: *"I am the vine, ye are the branches: He that abideth in me, and I in him, the same bringeth forth much fruit: for without me ye can do nothing" (John 15:5).*

Lesson Aim: The student will be able to name two of the three relationships the believer enjoys with Christ. The student will be encouraged to examine his own life to see if he enjoys these relationships.

Are You Ready?

The story is told of a young man who had fallen in love with a lovely young woman. They enjoyed each other very much. Often they would eat together at a restaurant or at the young woman's family home. On one such occasion, the young lady excused herself following the meal and went to the kitchen to do dishes and clean up the preparation mess. The young fellow liked this arrangement for it gave him time to read the paper, visit with her dad and relax. With a sly grin the father told the young man, "Enjoy it now, son, for it won't always be that way." The young man was not sure what was meant, but he soon found out.

Sometime later, the two were married. Upon returning from their honeymoon, they settled into their new apartment. Following dinner, the new bride called to her husband to come and help her with the cleanup. "But I never helped before!" he protested. "Yes, you are right, but you weren't family then, either."

What had changed? He still loved her and she him, but their relationship was different now. There are some good changes that happen to every person who comes into a marriage relationship. The same is true of a salvation relationship. As a member of God's family, there are new privileges, new help, a new resource. If you have become a Christian, you are related to Christ. We want to spend two lessons exploring our new relationship to Him. Get your Bible ready.

See for Yourself

We begin today in 2 Corinthians 5:17. Find the place in your Bible. Now, let us read it together. Ready? Let's read. "Therefore if any man be in Christ. . . ." The first phrase talks about being "in Christ." Can anyone tell me how that happens? Are you in Christ? How do you know?

What is true of you if you are in Christ? Look in our verse for the answer. You are a new creature. It doesn't mean a creature from outer space or from the slimy lagoon. It really means that you are a new creation—you are made over, made new. Old things, old ways, the old relationship of being God's enemy are all gone. You are now a new-made son of God. This new relationship is like belonging to a new family. You are now related to God—He is your Father and you are His son.

There are special relationships with Jesus Christ, also. One of these relationships is described in Ephesians 4:11-16. Open your Bible to that place. Verse 11 names different kinds of workers God gives to the Church. Name them. They are apostles, prophets, evangelists, pastors and teachers. Verse 12 explains what those special workers are supposed to do. Verse 15 tells Who is the Head or Leader giving directions to the Church. Read to find out Who it is.

Christ is the Head or the Leader of the Church. Christians

are called the Body, the members of the Church. There is no sense in having a leader if there are no individuals to lead or none who will follow. We are to receive direction and leadership from Christ if we are in Him. All believers together form the Body of Christ. Much can be accomplished by working together. What will happen if the Body doesn't listen to its Head? There will be confusion, duplication, things left undone. What will a wise member of the Body of Christ do? He will follow Christ and the leaders He gives to the Church. Christ is the _____ (Head), the Christians are the _____ (Body).

A second relationship is described in John 10:14 and 26–30. Open your Bible to that chapter and read the verses. Try to find the way Christ is described there and how Christians are described. Begin. What did you find? What is Christ described as? He is the Good Shepherd. What are the believers described as? They are sheep.

What does the Shepherd do in verse 14? He knows the sheep. In verse 27? He knows them and leads them. In verse 28? He gives them eternal life; they are kept in His hand; they are protected. Summarize what the Good Shepherd does. He knows His own and cares for them, now and forever. The sheep are safe in Christ. If you are in Christ you, too, are safe in Christ's care. You need not worry about your future destination—you will arrive safely in Heaven because Christ, the Good Shepherd, will see to it that you do. What a comfort to be safe and protected by the Good Shepherd! Christ is the _____ (Shepherd), we are the _____ (sheep).

Another relationship for the Christian is described in John. Open your Bible to chapter 15. Let us read together verses 1–6. "I am the true vine, and my Father. . . ." Jesus is talking here to the disciples. He is using another picture to describe how they are related to Him. What does Jesus call Himself in verses 1 and 5? He says, "I am the Vine." What does He call the disciples in verse 5? He says they are the branches. The word "abideth" means to remain or to stay.

What happenes to a branch that is cut or broken off the vine? It eventually withers and dies. What does the vine provide for the branch? It gives water, food and is its source of life. Without the vine the branch dies. As we stay close to Christ, drawing from Him strength and our very life, we will produce fruit.

Can grapes grow without a vine? No, they need the vine. Do branches grow grapes without the vine? No, they cannot. Can you see a similarity here to the life of a Christian? Would you explain what you see? Jesus said it very simply, "Without me ye can do nothing." We had best not get too puffed up thinking how good we are in ourselves. We need Christ to even live; He is our Source.

Christ is the _____ (Vine) and Christians are the _____ (branches).

Live It

Can you recall the relationships we studied? Fill in the missing spots below:

CHRIST	CHRISTIAN
HEAD	
	SHEEP
VINE	

(Answers, top to bottom: members or Body, Good Shepherd, branches) How about you? Are you related to Christ? Are you in Him? Is He in you? If not, you may come to be His today. Confess your sin and receive His death as payment for your sin.

Are you allowing Christ to be your Head? Do you follow His direction in your life or do you make all your own choices? He longs to "call the shots." Allow Him to have His rightful place.

Are you resting safely in Christ? As a Christian you should, you know. Don't worry, doubt or be anxious about eternal life. No one can take you from His strong hand once you are there.

Are you drawing strength from Him? Or are you trying to be an independent branch? You can't do anything that way. Abide—stay close to Him for strength and for truth.

To the Instructor: Make It Visual

Moody transparency #9 from *Basic Bible Doctrine #4* will beautifully illustrate this lesson. Use a blank sheet to mask off the chart of relationships, revealing one at a time as they are dealt with. For the review in the "Live It" section, prepare small slips of paper to block out the words indicated. Remove each one as it is recalled.

You may decide to draw your own diagram to illustrate each relationship. Use stick figures, teaching pictures or gather the real object (i.e., vine and branch). See idea below.

RELATED TO CHRIST
(Part 2)

Scripture Text: *"Therefore if any man be in Christ, he is a new creature: old things are passed away; behold, all things are become new" (2 Cor. 5:17).*

Lesson Aim: The student will be able to name two relationships that the Christian has with Christ. The student will be encouraged to examine his own life to see if he is allowing these to work for him.

Are You Ready?

Today we will continue our study of the new relationships that the Christian has with Christ. You will recall our study of the Head and the Body, the Shepherd and the sheep, the Vine and the branches. Before we proceed, listen to two short stories and discover why these children were treated differently.

One night Janice stayed over at Kelly's house. The next morning Kelly's mother made Kelly make her bed before school. However, she said nothing to Janice about her bed. What was the difference? Why didn't Kelly's mother make Janice do her bed?

Two young boys did well in the Friday spell-off. Geoffrey and Keith were the last two spellers left standing in the room.

When they went home that day to Keith's house to get a snack and to play, they told Keith's mom what had happened. Keith's mom smiled and gave her son a hug. She didn't hug Geoffrey. Why do you think she treated him differently?

In both stories the parents responded to their own child. They didn't have to, and didn't respond to the neighbor child. They were responsible for their own child, not the neighbor's boy or girl.

Are you related to Christ? If you are, He is responsible to protect you, to love you, to correct you, to provide for your every need.

See for Yourself

Please find 1 Peter 2:1–7 in your Bible. We will be reading and discussing it together. In verse 2, Peter tells what baby Christians will want. What is that? We will desire the sincere milk of the Word. That is another way to say that new Christians will want to read and study the Bible in the same way that newborn babies love to drink milk. Here Peter is talking about some of the "new things" that we read about last week in 2 Corinthians 5:17. ". . . In Christ . . . all things are become new."

Verse 3 says, "If so be" (if verse 2 is true of you), then "you have tasted [experienced] that the Lord is gracious." Verse 4 is still talking about Christ. How is He described here? He is called a Living Stone. Christ was rejected by men but chosen by God. Look at verse 5 to find what new believers are described as. What did you see? We are living stones, too. In verses 6 and 7, Christ is called the Cornerstone. A cornerstone is an important stone at the corner of two walls. It is supposed to be the beginning stone, the one that causes the others to be straight and level. When it is used to describe a person, it shows his importance. In the building process of a new building, a cornerstone is usually laid to give the year of the construction. Inside the cornerstone are stored valuable items, such as books and mementos relating to the building.

What do you think "Christ is the cornerstone" means? He gives Christians direction, a place of beginning. If we are stones, together we make a building for God. From our lives Christ wants to construct a building. We are to be a testimony for Christ, part of His building.

Christ is the Chief _____ (Cornerstone); Christians are _____ (living stones).

Open your Bible to Matthew 9:14 and 15. Jesus was with His followers, the disciples. Who came up to Him? The disciples of John the Baptist came to ask Jesus a serious question. What did they ask? They asked, "Why don't your disciples fast?" "Fasting" means to choose not to eat so that you may have more time to pray and read the Bible. Jesus' answer to their questions explains another relationship between Christ and believers. Listen carefully as we read it in verse 15. Who do you think Jesus called the children of the bride chamber? If you were thoughtful and careful, you chose the disciples of Jesus. Who would be the bridegroom? Jesus is the Bridegroom; the Christians are the Bride.

This is a confusing picture but it is spoken of in several places in the Bible. In Ephesians 5 where instructions are given to husbands and wives, this idea is used again. Each Christian alone is not a bride, but together with all Christians we form one bride, the Bride of Christ. Ephesians 5:25 says, ". . . as Christ loved the church and gave himself for it." The last book of the Bible tells about the wedding of the Bride which has not happened yet. Revelation 19:6–9 tells of the Bride, her marriage to Christ, and a supper to celebrate afterwards.

As our Groom, Christ loves us! He is determined to marry us—to take us to be with Him forever. He is in Heaven and so will we be.

Live It

Are you allowing Christ to be your Cornerstone? Is He setting the direction of your life, or are you? Are you part of His building—His testimony in the world? Or do you prefer to

155

"do your own thing"? He was chosen of God. Who are you to set Him aside?

Do you love Christ? Do you want to be with Him, near Him? Has your relationship grown to that point? He loves you more than you love anyone, even yourself.

"Therefore if any man be in Christ, he is a new creature: old things are passed away; behold, all things are become new" (2 Cor. 5:17).

To the Instructor: Make It Visual

The Moody Press transparency #9, *Basic Bible Doctrine #4* will help you review and present today's topic. If at all possible, bring some bricks and/or cinderblocks to demonstrate the cornerstone concept. A picture of a couple involved in a wedding will be useful to illustrate the second point. Discuss the reason for both illustrations as they relate to Christ.

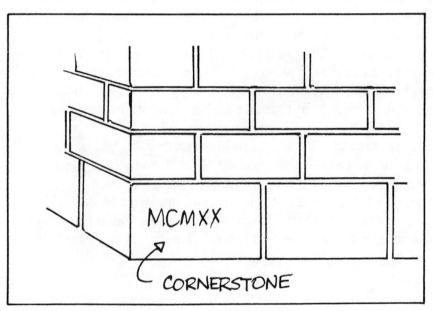

CHRIST'S PRESENT WORK

Scripture Text: *"For there is one God, and one mediator between God and men, the man Christ Jesus" (1 Tim. 2:5).*

Lesson Aim: The student will be able to name Christ's present work—mediation. The student will explain why Christ is a fit mediator and why there is only *one*.

Are You Ready?

We have learned about Christ's work at creation. We have studied carefully something of what His death meant for us. We have talked about ransom, reconciliation, propitiation and substitution. During one lesson we focused on proofs of Christ's resurrection, His coming back to life. We looked at His going up to Heaven, His ascension. Last time we considered the new relationships of a believer to Christ. See how many you can name from memory.

Christ is the Head of the Church, the Shepherd, the Vine, the Cornerstone, and the Groom. Christians are His Body the Church, the sheep, the branches, the living stones and the Bride.

Where is Christ today? Is He on earth as a man? No, we learned in Acts 1 that He went where? Yes, Christ is in Heaven today. Have you ever wondered what He is doing there? Do you know that what He does involves every Christian? The work He does there began here on earth before He left. There are clues in the Gospel of John and Acts. Let's take a look.

See for Yourself

Open your Bible to John 14. You may remember that this chapter is a conversation that Jesus had with the disciples. These events happened just hours before Jesus was crucified. These were His final words to His disciples. He had tried to warn them but they became frightened and confused. Read verses 1–6. What does Jesus say to them in verse 1? Use your own words. "Don't be worried," He tells them. Verse 2 tells what He is going to go away to do. What is that? He is going to make a place ready for them. Why does Christ prepare a place for these men in Heaven when they live on earth? He intended to bring them to Heaven because He wanted them to be with Him.

Jesus tells them that they know how to get where He is going. Thomas isn't so certain. What does he ask in verse 5? "How can we know the way if we don't even know where you are going?" Thomas is upset, no doubt. He wants to know, but he feels bewildered, left out, frustrated at the thought of losing Jesus. What is Jesus' reply to him and the others (v. 6)? He is going to His Father and He also says that He is the Way for others to get there. Access to Heaven, to God's presence, is through the Person of His Son, Jesus Christ. He is the Way between earth and Heaven. He is the Way from here to there.

Open your Bible to 1 Timothy 2:5. This verse will give us a name for the work of "going between" that Christ does. Read the verse for yourself. Can you find the word we are talking about? The word is "mediator." Can you pronounce it? Say it out loud three times to your neighbor.

In order for a mediator to work there must be two separate groups of people involved. Who are they here? One is God, the other is men. Describe the one God 1 Timothy 2:5 names. What is He like? Yes, He is powerful, He is wise, He is above everyone. He is holy—clean, pure, without error or wrong.

158

What is man like? Intelligent, limited, sinful, greedy.

What do you think would be good qualities of a go-between, a mediator, in any situation? He should be respected by both sides. He should be powerful enough to persuade each to consider the other's situation, needs and proposals. How does Christ Jesus qualify as a mediator in the conflict of sin between God and man?

Jesus was and still is God, so He knows God's viewpoint and perspective. Jesus was incarnated as a man; He has experienced what it is to be a man. He was hungry, tired, sad, distressed, attacked and tempted. He reveals God to us and presents us to God. But He also makes us presentable, acceptable. His death on the cross allows us to approach God. Just like John 14 says, He is the Way—He doesn't just point the way. His death and resurrection make the way to God and Heaven possible for all who believe in and receive Him.

How many "go betweens" are there according to our verse in 1 Timothy? How many? Are you sure? There is ONE, only ONE. Others may claim to be the way to God, but only Christ is the Truth and the Way. No other form of religion, no other prophet or man has power to bring us to God (Acts 4:12).

Christ's work in mediation is begun at the cross, but continues on as He pleads before God for others to have entrance to Heaven and to life eternal. He pleads for God to adopt us because of the work Christ finished (John 19:30). Hebrews 9:24 says Christ is entered ". . . into heaven itself, now to appear in the presence of God for us." He is in Heaven now. What is He doing? He is in the presence of God on our behalf—pleading for us. Look at Hebrews 7:25 and Romans 8:34. Both verses use the word "intercession." Christ is making intercession for us, presenting us to God. How often does He do this for believers? He is constantly doing it—it is His present work.

Live It

Do you believe that Christ will succeed at His work for

you? Why? He will succeed because He is God and all-powerful. It has nothing to do with who He pleads for. What do you think should be our part in all this? Can we help in the mediating? No, we cannot. Why not? We are sinful men—limited, fallen, sinful. We have no right to stand before God. Then what can we do?

We can realize what Christ does for us and we can be thankful for it. We can express our thanks in prayer, in service, in worship and in witness.

How about you? Are you trying to find your own way to God? "For there is one God, and one mediator between God and man, the man Christ Jesus" (1 Tim. 2:5).

To the Instructor: Make It Visual

Moody Press transparency #10 from *Basic Bible Doctrine #4* with the Jesus emphy is designed to reinforce this lesson. Read the instructions for effective use and visual impact.

The diagram below is a visual means to demonstrate the concept of mediator. It is added to as you progress, but is given here as a series for your convenience. You will find either a chalkboard or overhead transparencies which can be prepared ahead of time and used as overlays are most effective.

CHRIST'S FUTURE WORK

Scripture Text: *". . . The hour is coming, and now is, when the dead shall hear the voice of the Son of God. . . . And shall come forth; they that have done good, unto the resurrection of life; and they that have done evil, unto the resurrection of damnation" (John 5:25, 29).*

Lesson Aim: The student will be able to name Christ's future work (resurrection, judgment, ruling) and His role in each (snatching away believers, Judge, King).

Are You Ready?

Today is the final lesson in our series on Jesus Christ. A review quiz is provided to test your skills of memory. Answers are available when you are finished doing as much as you can alone.

We talked last time about Christ's work right now. What is it called? He is our Mediator. What does that mean? He is our Go-between before God. In what real place does Jesus do this work for believers? He is in God's presence in Heaven interceding for us. What reason does Christ give to God for receiving us? His, that is Christ's, death and resurrection provide our way to God. Is He interceding for you? The answer is yes if you are a believer. He is not interceding for you if you are trying to build your own way to God.

Christ has work yet to do. He has three major responsibilities in future events. While the Bible does not tell us the calendar day or year for these events, we do know many other details. We can be sure they will happen just as the Bible tells us they will.

We don't know when but we do know who is involved, how and, in many cases, where these events will be held. Ready for a discovery expedition? You will need your Bible as a guide.

See for Yourself

We will look at three major events where Christ is the central figure. Let's look to see if you and I will be involved, what will take place and what Christ will be doing.

First, open your Bible to 1 Thessalonians 4:13. This was a letter written to comfort Christians who had seen some loved ones die. Read with me through verse 18.

How were they to respond to the death of those in Jesus? They were not to sorrow the way others do who have no hope. Your loved one won't always be separated from you, Paul says. Verse 14 tells you of a future event. Can you tell which word(s) lets you know that? It says God *will* bring (them) with Him. "Will" is a future tense—an action not yet completed. Look at verse 15. Will all Christians be dead when this happens? How do you know? Some will be alive and still here on earth. Some will be dead. What does Christ our Lord do (v. 16)? He descends, that is, comes down from Heaven. Does He come quietly? No!! He shouts! He has an angel's voice, and a trumpet call will sound loudly announcing His coming. What will happen here on earth (vv. 16, 17)? Dead Christians will rise from the ground first. Then living believers will be caught up into the clouds. Sounds a lot like Acts 1 and Jesus' ascension, doesn't it? Where will all these believers go (v. 17)? They will meet the Lord in the air and be with Him in Heaven.

What do we call it when someone comes back to life? We

call it a resurrection. So the first event is a resurrection. Some call it the Rapture, which means "caught up." What two groups will be involved? (1) Dead Christians; (2) believers who are alive at that time. What does Christ do? He descends and snatches away all believers, dead and alive, from the earth.

For the second future event, open your Bible to John 5. This event is called the Tribulation. It means "the time of trouble." The book of Revelation has a longer description of it (Rev. 5—18) and its events. We want to get an overview of this seven-year period of great trouble. Since this event follows the first event, the Rapture, who will *not* be involved here? Why? Believers will not be included in the Tribulation because they are "with the Lord." By careful study it becomes clear that unbelievers will be involved in this time of trouble. Read John 5:22 to find out who is responsible for judgment. God the Father gives this task to His Son, Jesus Christ. How does Jesus have authority to be the Judge according to verse 27? God, Who has all power and authority in Heaven and earth, gives to the Son authority to do what is necessary. He makes Him the Judge.

What kind of a Judge is the Son (vv. 27, 30)? As the Son of Man, He will be acquainted and associated with those He judges. He, too, was a man. He is fair and just, giving out proper penalties for offenses. He is not trying to further Himself, nor does He have any selfish motive. He judges in behalf of God Himself, Who is always fair. What will the judgments be according to verse 29? They will be either life or damnation. Are there other choices? No, those are the only ones. It appears to be an either/or situation.

Who is involved in the Tribulation? Unbelievers. What does Christ do? He is the Judge, either giving them life or condemning them to death. Will any escape (v. 28)? No, all will be called to account.

The third event is described in Revelation 20:1–4. Open your Bible to that portion of Scripture and let's read it slowly together.

The first three verses talk of Satan's future. He will be bound, shut up in a pit with no bottom, and secured there for a thousand years. He will not be permitted to deceive any during that time. What kind of a scene is described in verse 4? A place with thrones, and rulers sitting on the thrones. Who else is present? Martyrs for the name of Christ are present, too. They are those who were not in Satan's following during the Tribulation. What happened to the martyrs and the Tribulation survivors and these rulers? They all lived and reigned. What does "reign" mean? It is another word for rule. It carries the idea of being over someone else, or having a place of responsibility. How long do they rule? They rule for a thousand years. Who do they rule with? Christ. What do you believe Jesus will do during that thousand years?

Take a look at 1 Corinthians 15:25. This verse is talking about Christ, too. What task is to be accomplished while He is the King? All enemies will be put under His feet. Psalm 110:1 says the same thing another way. Listen: "The LORD said unto my Lord, Sit thou at my right hand, until I make thine enemies thy footstool." There have been enemies of God in all times since Satan rebelled. At the time of the Kingdom, Christ will put them all in their proper place—under His control.

Live It

In the Resurrection/Rapture Christ will _____ (snatch away to Heaven) all believers, both dead and alive. Will you be involved? Are you a believer? If you are, then you will be a participant in this future event. You will go to be with Him forever! If you are not, you may be a participant in the second event. In the Tribulation, Christ will be the _____ (Judge) of unbelievers. He will be fair but will condemn to death all who have not received Christ. How would He have to judge you if the Tribulation were today?

Finally, in the Kingdom Age, Christ is the _____ (King). What will He do to all His enemies? He will put them under His rule. All who are His will rule with Him. All who

164

are His enemies (Col. 1:21) will be put into subjection. Will you rule? Or will you be put down?

These are true events. They will come to pass. Examine your heart to see if you are ready to receive what is coming to you . . . or come to Christ today! He wants you to.

To the Instructor: Make It Visual

The Moody Press transparency #C4 from *Basic Bible Doctrine* is vital here. Transparency #11 gives the lesson's topic in bold headlines. Each event is pictured on a separate emphy to be added as you arrive at each. The emphys can be removed and replaced again during the "Live It" review time.

Prepare a simple time line to show the sequence of these events you study today. A sample is below. You may find these symbols helpful to summarize Christ's role:

Rapture (⎍), Tribulation (⚖ Judge), and Kingdom (♔ King).

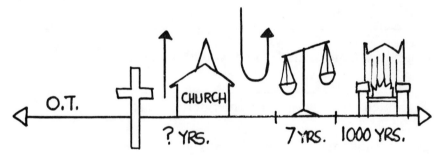

REVIEW

You will earn credit if you answer correctly 15 of the following 20 questions. Work carefully. Your teacher has the answer sheet.

1. Who is the Creator of everything? _____

2. What does "sustainer" mean? (a) Strong (b) Holds together (c) Trouble

3. The Incarnate Christ means _____

_____

4. What does Colossians 1:16 tell you about Jesus? _____

_____

5.—8. Match these words with their definitions:

_____ Ransom   A. To satisfy someone's anger

_____ Reconciliation   B. To take someone's place

    C. To set free

_____ Propitiation   D. To buy back

_____ Substitution   E. To bring together two enemies

9. Fill in the blanks:

Ye seek _____ who was _____. He is not here, for

_____ is _____, as He said (Matt. 28:5, 6).

10. What does "resurrection" mean? _____

11. Who saw Jesus after He was resurrected? _____

12. Who was with Jesus when He was taken up to Heaven? __

_____

13. What message did the angels give the disciples in Acts 1:10,

11? _____

14. When Jesus went to Heaven, who came to help the disciples?

_____

(Hint: They were to wait for Him in Jerusalem.)

15. Jesus is the Shepherd, Christians are _____
(John 10:11).

16. Christians are the Body of Christ, Jesus is the _____
(Eph. 4:15).

17. Jesus is the Vine, Christians are the _____ (John 15:5).

18. Today Jesus is our Mediator before God. What does Media-

tor mean? _____
(1 Tim. 2:5).

19. and 20. In the future time Jesus will do what in each event
listed?

    (a) Resurrection _____

    (b) Kingdom _____

EXTRA CREDIT: During the Tribulation (time of trouble)

Jesus will be _____

_____

Answers:

1. *Jesus*

2. *B*

3. *in the flesh—Jesus was in a body, He was a man*

4. *He made everything that is seen and invisible, too*

5. *D*

6. *E*

7. *A*

8. *B*

9. *Jesus   crucified   he   risen*

10. *To come back to life—alive*

11. *disciples, Mary and women, 500 men*

12. *disciples*

13. *This Jesus will come again*

14. *Holy Spirit*

15. *sheep*

16. *Head*

17. *branches*

18. *a go-between, middleman*

19. *bring Christians to Heaven*

20. *He will be King and rule the world*

Extra Credit: *our Judge—send trouble on unbelievers*